Edward Quaile

Illuminated Manuscripts

Their Origin, History and Characteristics

Edward Quaile

Illuminated Manuscripts
Their Origin, History and Characteristics

ISBN/EAN: 9783742814593

Manufactured in Europe, USA, Canada, Australia, Japa

Cover: Foto ©Thomas Meinert / pixelio.de

Manufactured and distributed by breboo< publishing software (www.brebook.com)

Edward Quaile

Illuminated Manuscripts

ILLUMINATED MANUSCRIPTS:

Their Origin, History and Characteristics.

A SKETCH,

BY

EDWARD QUAILE.

WITH TWENTY-SIX EXAMPLES FROM BOOKS OF
HOURS IN HIS POSSESSION.

LIVERPOOL:
HENRY YOUNG & SONS, SOUTH CASTLE STREET.
1897.

CONTENTS.

	PAGE.
LANGUAGE AND ART: WHENCE ARE THEY?	vii
ILLUMINATED MANUSCRIPTS: WHAT ARE THEY?	1
THEIR ORIGIN	5
THEIR USE BY EARLY CHRISTIANS	9
UNDER CONSTANTINE AND SUCCESSORS	13
UNDER CHARLEMAGNE AND HIS SUCCESSORS	19
STYLES OF ILLUMINATION PRIOR TO A.D. 1000:	
BYZANTINE	21
ANGLO SAXON	32
CARLOVINGIAN	49
STYLES OF ILLUMINATION SUBSEQUENT TO A.D. 1000:	
ITALIAN	60
FRENCH	68
ENGLISH	70
PRODUCTION OF ILLUMINATED MANUSCRIPTS	81
VALUE IN THE MIDDLE AGES	93
DESTRUCTION, VARIOUS CAUSES	99
ECCLESIASTICAL USE OF LATIN: ITS EFFECT AND INFLUENCE	106
BOOKS OF HOURS: WHAT THEY ARE	118
EXAMPLES OF THEIR ILLUMINATIONS	134
CONCLUSION	147

ILLUMINATIONS IN BOOKS OF HOURS REFERRED TO IN TEXT.

PLATES.		PAGE
I	*Obsecro te Domino*, as Hymn to the Virgin. French, about 1475. Coloured	*Frontispiece*
II	First page of a Calendar. French, about 1400 ...	136
III	St. John in Patmos. French, about 1400	139
IV	The same. French, about 1450	139
V	The same; also Expulsion from Eden. French, about 1475	139
VI	The Annunciation. French, about 1400	140
VII	The Annunciation. French, about 1425	140
VIII	The Annunciation, etc. (two pages). Flemish, about 1450	140
IX	The Annunciation, etc. (two pages). Italian, about 1475	141
X	The Annunciation, etc. (two pages). Italian (Sienna), about 1475	141
XI	The Visitation, etc. (two pages). Flemish, 1450 ...	141
XII	The Nativity, with the Wise Men on Journey. French, 1475	141
XIII	The Shepherds in the Fields, etc. (two pages). Flemish, 1450	142
XIV	Visit of the Wise Men. French, 1400	142
XV	Presentation in the Temple. French, 1516	142
XVI	Flight into Egypt. French, 1516	142
XVII	Coronation of the Virgin, etc. (two pages). Flemish, 1450	142

PLATES.		PAGE.
XVIII	*Obsecro te Domino.*, as Prayer to Virgin. French, 1400	143
XIX	*Stabat Mater.* French, about 1450	143
XX	David in Penitence. French, about 1475	143
XXI	Service for the Dead, in Church, at Vespers. French, about 1450	143
XXII	Battle Scene. French, 1475	143
XXIII	Descent of the Holy Ghost. French, about 1450	143
XXIV	Burial of Christ. French, about 1400	144
XXV	Saints Peter and Paul. French, about 1400	144
XXVI	Death and Ascension of the Virgin. Italian, about 1500	145

INTRODUCTION.

LANGUAGE AND ART: WHENCE ARE THEY?

AN official in one of our Cathedrals is stated* to have described himself as being the "dean's Verger," and that his duty was "to supersede the dean when he goes to his stall." The few words now employed about language and art is to do, for the matter in hand, what the verger meant was his duty to the Dean, to precede and clear the way.

The Greeks, among other legends, about the origin of language, had one that writing was a gift that came down from heaven, ready formed; and savages on seeing its use for the first time have acted as if the paper were alive, and possessed the power of sight and speech. Max Muller says, "We cannot tell as yet what language is. It may be a production of nature, a work of human art, or a divine gift. If it be a production of nature, it is her last and crowning production, which she reserved for man alone. If it be the work of human art, it would seem to lift the human artist almost to the level of a divine creator. If it be the gift of God, it is God's greatest gift; for through it God spake to

* *Spectator.*

man and man speaks to God, in worship, prayer, and meditation." Another says, "The art impulse in itself is a continual and insoluble mystery, traceable from the earliest ages of man as an unaccountable desire to express and register what we love—beauty."

It goes without saying that air and water are God's gifts, and are for all living things. Language and art are not less but equally His gifts, though they are for man alone, and do not come in concrete form like air and water, but through agencies, some human, which are themselves gifts.

Language is a power, the interaction of various agencies, by which humanity expresses wants, desires, and emotions. It does so in two ways, by speech acting through sound, by writing acting through signs. Art has part in both. It is aid to spoken, and it is the first stage, the root from which written language has sprung. To Adam, the first of our race, powers came at once complete and perfect, but to all his descendents they come slowly and gradually. Spoken language, in its simplest form, is dependent:—*first*, on an atmosphere we call sound; *second*, an ear, for the reception and increase of sound; *third*, a brain for its assimilation; and *fourth*, a voice, with all that it includes, for its production. The atmosphere, with waves of ether, varied in form, elastic and mobile; the ear, with resonators and drums; the brain, with cells; the throat, with cords, each wonderful in its mechanical powers and workings, all these seem made for, as they interlock each other, and are necessary for speech. When they exist, in due proportion—meet, and, as it were, kiss each other—is there the ideal human voice, having an influence upon life, like wind upon water. In infancy it is a toy, in adult life an instrument of pleasure, a lever having power, equally in simple prose as in rhetoric, poetry, and music. Written language is even more wonderful, its power is not limited by distance or time, it carries messages to the antipodes, as it has brought them from ages long past, and will convey them from the present to those yet to come.

The first stage of writing was pictures, the possibilities of making which is owing to various gifts, such as light and sight.

The sublime dictum, "Let there be light," drew aside a veil and revealed the beauty existing in all nature, and the gift of sight brought that beauty home to man, through what has been called the "window of the soul," the eye, which, like the voice, is one of the gifts that soonest come and longest stay. With the first breath of life the voice awakes, the eye opens, and light enters, creating wonder, giving delight, shewing beauty. All act the part assigned to them by their Author until He wills they retire, and the drama of earthly life to end. In addition to various powers man is endowed with desires, aspirations and impulses, of which a delight in what is called beauty is as marked as it is universal. To possess anything in which it exists, to reproduce or retain it is ever an object. The delight never ceases, the impulse to obtain, renew, or create is never lost, but re-appears in every new generation, with the regularity of the seasons, and through powers of eye, hand and brain, and a few pigments, he succeeds in bringing up and exhibiting on a plane surface forms and colours in which beauty exists. To the young, such creations or pictures are always agreeable, and the attempts to produce them are constant, nor have we any more sufficient reason than that there is an impulse and a pleasure in the effort. The history of writing shews that pictures emanating from that impulse, and at first produced aimlessly, were soon found to be an aid to speech, or in lieu of speech. Indeed, to all peoples they were the first step to written language, some never had any other; the next being to make part of a picture serve for the whole, and the third to adopt signs that would stand for or recall thoughts or ideas that were intangible and without form. In time sufficient signs, or skeleton pictures, accumulated to form a mode of communication, convenient and valuable because available when the voice was inadequate.

Such, then, is the path by which art and language, spoken and written, have reached the only creature that possesses the wonderful gifts. Much more might be said, and yet leave questions regarding them unanswered. Even what has been said could be dispensed with, by whoever believes in the revelation that "man was formed in the image of his Maker." Brief as this declaration is, and simple as it seems, it includes and explains, as not any thing else can, man's delight in beauty and the possession of gifts and powers as well as his pleasure in their exercise. That exercise has had for results, not only art and language, but great achievements in science, which, though relatively only shadows, outlines, and imitations of Creation, are yet proofs and credentials of man's origin and his relationship to the one Infinite and Eternal Creator, as they are also warrant that to the gifts and powers possessed in this mortal life has been joined a heritage in one that is immortal.*

* Tennyson says—
"Thou madest man, he knows not why,
He thinks he was not made to die,"

While Dean Church considers that man's possession of the sense of beauty is a witness to his immortality, saying, "There is a mysterious endowment given to man—the sense of beauty, seen in much that address themselves to eye or ear, or to the inward mind or soul. Endlessly various in form and colour, in feature and expression, in voice and tone and ordered sound, and in all that is called into invisible existence by the powers of feeling and imagination—it comes before the human soul as one of the chief sources of its brightness, one of the chief things that exalt and gladden life—the spring within us which never dries up—admiration, delight, and rapture. Is it not our love and admiration of what is beautiful which points forward to the glory which shall follow—that the mysterious longing of our nature shall then be, as everything there is, pure, completed, enduring?"

ILLUMINATED MANUSCRIPTS:
What are They?

"There were brave men before Agamemnon," and there were books produced centuries before the earliest printers were born. "Oh, that mine adversary had written a book" was an exclamation in that far-away time, when the writing was the book, and the book was the writing, but now the writing is only the first step, and the name and status of a book is never attained at all, unless it has the aid of printer and publisher.

The books produced before, or without, printing are now called "Manuscripts"—one kind, "Illuminated Manuscripts," which is a title correct enough, and perfectly understood by those who deal in them, or possess them, but "caviare to the general," most of whom need the information that such are ancient books, which receive their name, and owe their present value, to having ornaments and pictures on them. Only highly esteemed books were so treated, and the value of all books, to which they were applied, was greatly increased and made more acceptable as a present, and desirable as a possession. Nothing mechanical had share in the production of them, but every line of the text, and outline of the design, every touch of colour, or gleam of gold, that "illuminated" and brightened them, was traced and applied by human eye and hand. This gives them a special interest to our times, which may be three, or thirteen hundred years, distant from those of their production.

Many of the earliest and most important of these manuscripts are now in public collections, carefully guarded as national treasures, and few know them from personal examination, or otherwise than from description, or reproduction in various printed works.

There are about fifty thousand manuscripts of one kind or another in the British Museum, and about one thousand of them are illuminated. In one of the halls of that wonderful institution a valuable selection of them is on view, an open page of each, protected by glass, showing an example of the illuminations that adorn them. The number in private hands in England it is difficult to estimate—Lord Crawford says it is large compared with Spain, Italy, or France—but as can be understood such are rarely seen out of the owner's possession. The illuminated manuscripts to be now considered were produced between the fourth and seventeenth centuries, in every country that accepted Christianity. They are the outcome of it, and are mainly of the writings in which its principles are embodied, explained, or applied. The ornamentations and illustrations added to these writings originated and sprung from the feeling that honour and veneration are due, and should be rendered, to what is sacred and divine, and many under that influence were done by members of religious communities as a religious and pious duty, as well as from the delight that beauty gives. Yet neither all Christians, nor all Christian communities, looked on the matter in exactly the same light. There were some of both, from the earliest times, who considered illuminations upon the sacred writings might be carried to excess, far beyond what they permitted, and in the use of pictures or decorations approached an irreverence, or even an idolatry, that those writings strongly condemned.

During the hundred and fifty years between A.D. 700 and 850 these opinions were dominant at Constantinople, the centre of power and civilisation, and throughout the Eastern Empire, of which it was the capital, resulting in a great destruction of these manuscripts and great discouragement to other forms of Christian art. Six hundred years afterwards the same ideas prevailed in parts of Western Europe, especially in Britain, and led to the same result. The consequence is that of the many examples that must have been produced prior to A.D. 1000, comparatively few remain, and those before 700 may be counted on the fingers.

Of what do remain before A.D. 1000 a considerable proportion were either produced in Britain, or on the Continent by British scribes, or under British influence. After that, the illuminations on manuscripts were more frequently the work of lay artists, and were not so exclusively as before applied to devotional books, but also to Chronicles, Romances, Poetry, Astrology, etc. In the early period it was the Gospels, Bibles and Psalters that were most frequently illuminated, among books of devotion, afterwards it was Books of Hours.

The illuminated manuscripts most frequently met with now in booksellers' catalogues are these Books of Hours, and were produced in France and Flanders. English ones are much more rare owing to the destruction already named, and also that when Books of Hours became more generally in use than either Psalter or Bible, England had greatly ceased to produce illuminated manuscripts. In the first period a good many of the sacred writings are in Greek, in the second they are mainly in Latin.

Illuminations seemed to begin by the initial letter of a chapter or other division of the book being given a marked importance through peculiar form or different colour. In time these initial letters, when the shape allowed it, had small pictures painted within them, which were then said to be "historiated," and looked like impressions from a seal, which may have suggested them.

Pictures were also indented in the borders or made to occupy more or less of an entire page. As the whole, both the writing and decoration, is by hand, each manuscript has a certain individuality, and, as a rule, comes like an original work, so far as the decoration is concerned. Of course these decorations differ much both in quantity as well as quality. A breviary or gospel, intended for a priest or a poor student, may be plain or with only a few capitals, while for a cardinal or archbishop, or for use in the service of a cathedral, it may contain a hundred or more illuminations, and may be on purple vellum, written in gold and silver letters, and adorned and enriched with all that skill or wealth could add to make it worthy the acceptance of king or emperor, or of a place on the altar. In many cases the fineness of the parchment, the blackness of the ink, the abundance and variety of the illuminations, and the brilliancy of the colours employed, claim our admiration and, combined with other points of interest, explain the charm these manuscripts possess. That history repeats itself is only a way of saying that man always acts in one way when circumstances are the same. There is, however, not any probability that there ever again can be such a combination of circumstances as originated and gave proportions to the production of illuminated manuscripts during the first fifteen centuries of the Christian era. Some of these circumstances must now be noted.

Their Origin.

The attempt to make pictures, or representations, is evidently an impulse not evolved by time, but natural to humanity, not confined to race, nor limited to age or ages, but seen equally in the ways and efforts of childhood, the remains of prehistoric man—cave-dwellers—as among uncivilised races now existing, who possess neither letters nor written language. Denis says: "It is with paintings on manuscripts, as well as with several branches of art and archæology, that the deeper may be the study, the greater may be the knowledge, only serves to place their origin earlier, puts it further and further back, from age to age, and the beginning seems to recede until the point is reached when the divine law was given."

Various writers on Egypt and China tell us that the written languages of those nations contain internal and visible evidence that they originated in pictures.*

The Mexicans and North American Indians recorded events entirely by pictures, and no doubt is entertained but that both were on the road to possessing a written language, when progress was stayed, by their national existence being ended, through foreign enemies.†

It is generally held that the world is indebted to the Phœnicians for the discovery or adoption of the letters now used. It is quite natural to think so because, being the greatest shipmasters and traffickers, perhaps manufacturers also, of their time, they would need or require them more than any nomadic or pastoral people, and be very ready to see their value and to adopt them, if invented by others, just as with us it is mainly because of our extensive colonies and

* Dr. Bridge says: "The Egyptians did not *write*, in our restricted sense; they *drew*; every letter was a picture of natural objects, more or less conventionalized. In fact, every Egyptian book may be said to be illustrated, for its text illustrates itself."

† When the Spaniards arrived on the coast of Mexico, advice and information was sent to the Emperor Montezuma, in the form of large paintings on cotton cloth, on which the ships, with their riggings, the Spaniards with their horses, arms, and artillery, were delineated. The native Mexicans continued to represent everything that had shape by natural forms, and ideas by characters that had some apparent connection.

The North American Indians had much the same mode of communication. Starting on a journey, the direction was represented by a bird taking flight; travelling on land, by a foot; on water, by a canoe. War was represented by a hatchet; peace, by a pipe; the slain, by heads; prisoners, by figures erect. The time of day was represented by the sun; of the month, by the quarter of the moon; of the year, by some figure associated with the particular month. Numbers they reckoned by tens, for which they had a figure not unlike ours.

commerce that we need, and in our language actually possess, more words than any other modern people. The probability is that to various communities, in different localities, without any connection, the value of signs or letters became apparent and were simultaneously used, for recent discoveries would show that they were known, and in use, by the islanders of Crete before they were by the Phœnicians. To what extent the latter invented or improved them it may not be possible to say, excepting that the practical use of letters came from them to the Greeks, and from the Greeks to the Romans, who passed them on to ourselves, or other Western peoples. Of the Greeks we do not know every step, but it was by the same road as other nations, though more rapidly, that they arrived at possessing a remarkable language and literature, to which the rest of the world has ever since been a debtor. We know, however, that long before the Christian era, art was present and applied by them to everything. The remains of paintings on walls and vases, the engravings on metals and precious stones, and the figures modelled in clay or chiselled in marble or other materials, all conclusively show this. Not any books of that early period, with pictures or illuminations upon them, remain to us, for reasons that will be noted hereafter, but we may be certain that art was applied by them to their books, as to other things, in the time of Alexander, from the fact noted that they had three words—"cryptography," which meant rapid or quick writing; "calligraphy," which meant ornamental or picture writing; and "chrisography," which meant writing in gold letters. There is also the fact noted, that one of their eminent painters, Pamphile, laid it down as a rule, that all children should learn to draw before entering on any other study.*

Pliny mentions, almost incidentally, that the Romans had illuminated books in the time of the Republic, and he and Cicero both describe several existing in their time; while Middleton thinks there is abundant evidence that they were common among the Romans of the Imperial period. That time, the "Augustan age," we know was proverbial as a period when art and literature were encouraged, when philosophers, orators, and poets of the highest rank flourished, when aqueducts, viaducts, roads, bridges, and buildings of all kinds, decorative and useful, were constructed, proving the existence of much taste, knowledge and engineering skill. The existence and practical application of much secular and material knowledge was a striking contrast with the crude ideas prevalent regarding a first cause,—divine power and worship being attributed and given to almost everything, even to insects and plants. That ideas, immature and childish, should dominate such an intellectual and masterful people seems strange, but being so, partly explains and throws a lurid light on the prevalent immorality and sensuality and the universal indifference to human life which seems to have then rivalled that of the darkest part of the "dark continent" in our own time.

* Laborde says this excellent system gave to Greece more artists than writers, as well as a public able to appreciate the creations of an Apelles or a Phidias.

Their Use by Early Christians.

It was in an age of such contrasts that Christianity appeared, not offering nor showing, either to Greek or Roman, anything new or better in art, scholarship, or mechanical knowledge, but making known what the greatest intellects of either peoples did not know, and seemed unable to discover, yet which even the simple, as well as the learned among them, could see was a reasonable, yet dignified idea, both of the Author of all, as of His greatest work—man, and the duty and objects of life. Of the progress and influence throughout the extensive empire of Rome, by the working of these ideas, and the spread of this knowledge, we are concerned only with their influence on art, especially the illumination of manuscripts.

Excepting Egyptian papyri, which are not in question, nearly all the illuminated manuscripts remaining were produced during the Christian era, and are of Christian writings. It is not intended, however, to say that pictures and ornaments were only added to such books, and within that time. It is certain that pictures preceded the signs evolved from them, that we call writing, and that Art in its highest form existed, and was applied to books before Christianity. But we wish to point out that it gave new subjects to art, and changed the direction and objects of art. With the Greeks, and their scholars the Romans, to represent beauty in form and colour was the aim and end, the all-in-all, of art. When Christians took up and used art, it was to make ideas new, dignified, solemn, more intelligible, more real and impressive, and the form which Christianity afterwards assumed, especially in the West, and the power it obtained, accounts for the encouragement in many ways it gave to art, through buildings and their decorations, books and their illuminations, and the ceremonial and accessories of an elaborate and striking ritual.

The first adherents of Christianity, and the first teachers and preachers, were poor men, but as the father of John the Apostle had hired servants; Luke was a physician—possibly also a painter; Matthew one of the class of tax farmers, who were generally rich; Paul [*] probably belonged to a family of wealth and importance—as he certainly in intellect was head and shoulders above most of his compeers; Nicodemus, Joseph of Arimathea and others, incidentally alluded to, such as Herod's steward and members of Cæsar's household, all showed that even from the first there was a sprinkling that had means and position. In accepting Christianity, not only were they risking all, but devoting all their means and powers to its service, and as the books and writings were highly valued as the charter of their faith and hope, and were needed by teachers, preachers and churches, a portion of the time, labour and money of the brethren would from the first be given to producing copies of

[*] That Paul was a tentmaker did not indicate a humble position, but was owing to the rule of the Jews that all must learn a trade. He obtained his learning under Gamaliel and others, but his intellect was inherited, as was also some wealth obtained, late in life, from his family, which had previously cast him off—owing to his conversion—but could not prevent him, owing to Jewish law, receiving his inheritance.

them, more than of any other writings by other bodies or communities then existing.

To extend Christianity was a duty and obligation on all accepting it, and the increase of members would increase not only the number of the sacred writings, but the value and use of pictures as effective in bringing the wonderful incidents before the eyes of the listeners. At no period of life, and among no people we have ever heard of, or know at this day, is there not a delight in pictures, especially in those to whom writing is unknown; and they must have been especially so then, to the inhabitants of Greek and Roman cities, who were generally surrounded with many representations of what was beautiful, in form and colour, and accustomed by shows, processions and triumphs to derive pleasure and amusement, and even what knowledge they possessed of events happening in the great world outside their own little circle. Very likely, in the preaching of the early Christians, whether in upper rooms, "with doors shut for fear of the Jews," or in the catacombs or other places of secret meeting, the voice and gesture would be the only means employed to bring up or illustrate their version of some of the dramatic incidents of which the Bible is full, and of more interest, to peoples who hear them for the first time, than Homer was to the Greeks, or the *Thousand and One Nights* to the Arabs. But when the audience was imperfectly informed, or entirely ignorant,—which would happen in some part of that wide empire into which Christianity had penetrated,—pictures would be used to bring incidents home and fix them on the memory. In later times we know some were used in the churches, as explanatory and supplementary to the reading, which was not in the language "understanded of the people;" while permanent paintings on the windows, frescoes on the walls, or mosaics on the ceilings, were what all could understand, when few could read, and while adding to the dignity and solemnity of the place, carried on a teaching when the voice was still.*

For about three hundred years after the introduction of Christianity by Paul into Rome, despite discouragement and persecution, there was an increase in the number of its adherents, and consequently of copies of the sacred writings, with or without ornament. Greek and Roman scribes and artists were abundant, for any demand beyond what Christians, who gave their service as of duty and love, could supply. On Constantine's accession there was a great change, and from being the religion of a despised or persecuted body, it became that of the state. Consequently the books in which its origin, history and principles were recorded became an object of curiosity, of interest, and venera-

---

* Denis says: "At the time when the ability to read was so restricted that the clergy alone possessed it, Menologues, covered with paintings, which artists had specially designed, were unrolled from the pulpit before the people, and, taken as truths, confirmed by their assistance the spoken words, and the eager eyes of the multitude followed in these figures the course of events, in the variety of the parables, and the grandeur of the narrative, which those who were able could strengthen by reading. In these times the windows of cathedrals, splendidly ornamented, show that painting was a permanent teaching, as the MSS. elaborated so patiently in the cloisters, were, in their way also, of the most solemn verities."

tion to a much greater number of people, and the production of them consequently greatly increased, as there was increased encouragement given to missionary efforts, which the excellent roads and security throughout the empire greatly facilitated. The change of religion by Constantine was specially marked by his leaving Rome.

Under Constantine and his Successors.

That Constantine should change his religion was less strange than that he should change his capital—leave a city which had been the theatre of incidents, and was filled with evidences and memories of all that has influence over the feelings and imagination, and found a new one.

Only a man with strong opinions and of strong will would have thought of making such a change, and there must have been strong reasons impelling him, in face of the objections that must have been present, and the opposition which the change must have evoked. Personal glory no doubt was not absent, the policy or need for having a more central and convenient capital, and a more suitable language for so widely extended an empire, was most likely present, and the remarkable beauty of the site had an influence, but probably the new religion, which so much enlarged his views and increased his responsibilities, was the chief motive. If he had adopted Christianity in all sincerity, truly believing in its divine origin, and its civilising tendency, he must have considered its adoption would be a great benefit to his empire, and therefore to establish it, help it forward, and secure its permanency, would be an object of supreme importance.

To succeed in these he probably saw would be most difficult in Rome, every stone in which was pagan, and in which had grown up and hardened not only memories, but interests that might well seem to him immovable. The site which Constantine chose was in a locality where the language current, Greek, was that of the learned world of the time, a language more easily learned, and so more suited for a wide empire, than Latin. The Bible had been translated into it for five hundred years, and it was the one in which the gospels * and epistles were written. Christianity had early been preached there, and a considerable number of adherents already existed: so not only was opposition not to be feared, but the change of religion was in harmony with religious beliefs already accepted, and the change of capital was cause for rejoicing, as promising material advantages. The site chosen had for a thousand years borne the name of Byzance, and its possession of noted temples, the existence of medals struck there, and the names of sculptors and painters born there, are evidences that it was no mean city.

It had suffered more than many other Greek cities from the Romans, and the Christians there, as elsewhere in Asia, had been persecuted. But both art and Christianity were living when Constantine chose it for a capital, and strove to make it worthy the mighty empire of which he was head. Rome, which was deserted, did not become Christian; nor,

* That by St. Matthew was written in Hebrew.

despotic, strong-minded, and masterful, as Constantine was, could he by decree make it so. When he left Rome, the Senate maintained the old religion as before, continued to erect pagan altars, to vote money for the support of pagan worship, to elect pagan officials, to retain only pagan festivals in the calendar, and, on his death, Constantine was by it deified and placed among the gods: in this following the course adopted with the emperors, before Christianity was acknowledged, and as would have been continued had it never existed.

And pagan Rome continued, during the reign of several of the successors of Constantine, Christians increasing in numbers, but Christianity losing more and more of its distinctive difference, until when the city adopted it, so many of the old beliefs and practices were retained, that the change seemed mainly in name.*

Constantine having determined the site, removed from Rome to his new capital what he thought would add to its importance or magnificence, or in keeping with its rank, as the first, in every sense, of Christian cities—making such additions as were required or consistent with that position, or with the new state of things. Among others he founded the Christian temple of Saint Sophia and established a

* Augustine wrote: "When peace was made, the crowd of pagans who were anxious to embrace Christianity were deterred by this,—that whereas they had been accustomed to pass the festivals in drunkenness and feasting before their idols, they could not easily consent to forego these most pernicious, yet ancient pleasures. It seemed good then, to our leaders, to favour this part of their weakness—and for these festivals which they relinquish, to substitute others, in honour of the holy martyrs, which they might celebrate with similar luxury, but not with the same impiety."

library, which, at his death, contained six or seven thousand volumes. He also caused fifty copies of the Bible to be written and sent to various parts of the empire.*

The removal from Rome of what was desirable was continued by the successors of Constantine, especially Justinian, who rebuilt the cathedral of Saint Sophia, after its destruction by fire, much as it now remains, and added greatly to the artistic treasures of the city—"statues, pictures, illuminated books were there in heaps."

Constantinople was not only the great city, but the learned city, where art and learning flourished, being understood, appreciated and encouraged by a luxurious court and wealthy amateurs. Artists were required, and the art of Greece was turned into a new channel. The sacred writings supplied new ideas and abundance of subjects, ornament and elaboration applied to everything at that court was also bestowed on the books so highly esteemed. But in time ornaments and illustrations, pagan in idea, form, or symbol, were used upon them which were objectionable, even impious to the eyes and understanding of those who read the sacred writings in their own tongue, without gloss or interpretation.

For fully one hundred years there were complaints and written remonstrances,† but in A.D. 724 came action. Leo,

---

* One of these, believed to be the only one remaining, was in recent times obtained for the Emperor of Russia, from the convent on Mount Sinai, to which it had probably been given by its founder, the Emperor Justinian.

† Among others, Xenias, Bishop of Heliopolis, and Serenas of Marseilles; while St. Jerome said, "Let who like keep old books written in gold on purple vellum—burdens they are, rather than books. Give me and mine what is simple, valuable for accuracy rather than beauty."

called the Isaurian, at that time reached the throne, carrying to his high position ideas, sympathies, or prejudices acquired in the position of shepherd boy and simple soldier, from which he had risen, as doubtless they represented the traditional preaching and teaching of Paul and his successors "throughout all Asia." At any rate, Leo issued an order for the destruction of images which were worshipped or used in worship, and also of books in which were pictures or ornaments derogatory to, or inconsistent with, or opposed to scriptural teaching. At this time the library, founded three hundred years before, contained about 100,000 volumes, one half being Christian writings, the other half the best examples of ancient authors. Many were splendidly ornamented, some of the most magnificent in the world. Among them were examples belonging to previous emperors, written on purple vellum in letters of gold or silver. This library was set on fire, and half the number of the books it contained perished, especially those containing Christian pictures,. among them being a copy of Homer, considered the finest example of Greek chrysography ever seen, and the loss of which is still deplored. Beyond the books in this state library there were many in private possession which, partly for fear and a desire for favour, were burnt also. That Leo in this act was in accord with opinion, as far as any can be said to exist, is probable, because twenty years afterwards— in A.D. 754—a convention of over three hundred bishops approved of the proceedings and action, and at a meeting in the great square of Constantinople, the assembled people were sworn on a naked cross and a copy of the Gospels, without ornament, that images of holy persons offered for worship should be considered as idols and treated as such. With the exception of slight intervals, these ideas were dominant wherever the Eastern Emperors had influence or power to enforce them, with the result that the number of books, statues, and other forms of Christian art destroyed during that period was greater than by the barbarians in Italy. Not only were such things given to the flames, but often the artists who produced them with them. In Rome, however, or wherever the Pope had influence, not only was there refusal to follow on these lines, but excommunication was threatened by Gregory II, Pope at the time, on whoever would attempt to carry out Leo's orders. This was quite to be expected from what has been said of the Christianity of Rome, being so much imbued with Paganism. That ideas should exist differing so much from those in the East and receive support, must, in no small degree, have been owing to the act of Constantine in changing the capital. In deserting Rome, and leaving the throne of the Cæsars vacant, he was making an opening, almost inviting an occupant, and providing support for claims of precedence and superiority, both spiritual and temporal, which were afterwards made.

When Paul came to Rome, and long after, the imperial religion was practically the worship of the divine majesty of Rome, incarnate in human form, in the series of the Emperors, especially the reigning one, who was the religious head—*Pontifex Maximus*, the "Supreme Pontiff"—so, when the bishop of Rome became Pope, and the Pope temporal prince, he took, in addition to those from his Christian office of bishop, various imperial titles which, to the multitude at the time, especially of Rome and Italy, seemed less an usurpation or invention than the natural appanage belonging to one who possessed the capitol, sat on the seat of the Cæsars, and used their very language.*

Under Charlemagne and his Successors.

While the destruction of illuminated manuscripts and statues was going on by Iconoclast Emperors of the East, there was a great contrast in the West by the encouragement given to art and literature by Charlemagne, whose efforts, it is strange to think, were successful by the aid of scholars and teachers not from Rome or Constantinople, but from that most distant point of the Roman Empire the natives of which were spoken of by Virgil as quite outside the civilised world—"*Ex penitos to diviso orbe Britannos.*" The grandson of Charles Martel, who arrested the career of the Saracens in Europe, the son of Pepin, who welded various tribes into one kingdom of Franks, and made also the Pope a temporal sovereign, Charlemagne was the most remarkable man of his time—one of any time. Endowed with physical and

* "Caligula was the first who offered his foot to be kissed, and the first who claimed divine honours for himself, and had a temple and a priest, with victims, in honour of his divinity. The Pope, in the ceremonial of presentation, requires each to bow the knee nine times, and to kiss his slipper. In this act he recalls, and it seems prefers to consider himself, rather the successor of the pagan Emperor and *Pontifex Maximus*, than of the Fisherman-Apostle, Peter."

mental qualities, he was enabled to control and rule the turbulent natives of his inherited possessions, and to add to them those of Italy and Germany. Having an innate delight in art and learning, he fostered and encouraged them both in every way possible. While a supporter of the Pope's temporal power, which his father had created and he consolidated, and many of his spiritual claims, he was yet opposed to the worship of images, but not to the use of art in aid of religion and education. His opposition to the worship of images was mainly political, to prevent the Emperor of Constantinople exercising any power in the West.* Like Constantine, he founded a capital—Aachen. Aix-la-Chapelle—and brought there from other places, artistic treasures of all kinds, and gathered round him strangers such as could assist him in giving light and learning to his subjects.†

The most remarkable among them was a native of York—Alcuin—who, in all connected with the beginning of art and learning in France, is always associated with Charlemagne, as

* "Charles, of course, could not endure that the Pope should be in vassalage to his political rival of the East, and was, moreover, an abominator of image-worship. Whatever languid eastern Christians might do, the independent Franks would never prostrate themselves in abasement before the effigies of saints."—ALCUIN. WEST.

† Many years ago, while under the glamour of his striking personality, I visited this capital, where he was buried, with one of the illuminated manuscripts he loved so well on his knees, and afterwards stood, with emotion, on the Rhine in the room, hardly larger than the one in which this is written, where his grandsons, in A.D. 843, met to divide his great kingdom between them,—one taking France, another Italy, and another Germany. This, to me, dwarfed even the visit to the same place, five hundred years afterwards, by our Edward III, who may have been influenced by this previous event to fix a meeting there with the Emperor of Germany, in support of his claims on the throne of France.

his name has ever been held there in high honour. Learned in all the learning of the time, an enthusiast in all relating to its value and that of art, his life was spent in efforts for their advancement, both as pleasant in itself and a duty to humanity. His labours, and that of others from Britain, by the aid and encouragement of Charlemagne and his immediate successors, established monasteries in which were produced in France the first illuminated manuscripts worthy of the name, and the best for several centuries, and initiated a system of national education, the first in Europe.

Perhaps this is the place to consider various illuminated manuscripts, still existing, which were produced before his time, and for two hundred years afterwards, up to A.D. 1000. French writers class such under the heads of "Byzantine," "Anglo-Saxon," and "Carlovingian."

STYLES OF ILLUMINATION PRIOR TO A.D. 1000.
BYZANTINE.

Browne said, and Ruskin repeats, "Nature is the Art of God." The art of man is an effort to imitate nature—an impluse to create or to exercise the power to create. Man received the impulse and the power as heritage with the image of his maker, of which they are proofs and credentials. All peoples have had some kind of art and some kind of religion, generally accompanying and aiding each other. Man's endowments have enabled him to attain excellence in art, but a knowledge of the Giver of those endowments is only through His revelations. Any religion not based on or directed by that knowledge, has ever been childish or degrading. When Christianity, not by force but by intellectual, moral, and spiritual influences, dominated and displaced the religion of Greece and Rome, the art possessed by those peoples was directed into other channels, supplied with other subjects and motives.

It was at the time and through the act of Constantine in changing his religion and capital, that was the beginning of the artistic phase which, in the reign of Justinian, took form and crystalized in the style known as Byzantine, which influenced every other style in the West, and has not yet lost its power.

It was the successor, or rather was, Greek art modified by Christianity. A French writer marks the style as a transition from that of the ancients, which sought to give expression to beauty of form, and Christian art, the object of which was to make visible, and give form and life to an idea. Byzance, from which it took its name, was a city founded about 700 B.C. by one Magara, who led a colony from Cicily, the civilization of which, at that time, was equal to the rest of Greece. Owing to that, and its exceptional position, which Chateaubriand says "is the finest in the world," (and Napoleon, "it ought to be the capital of the world"), Byzance soon attained among cities rank and reputation.

The Christian religion was early introduced, and preaching, by Paul or his followers, heard in its streets. Its artists were capable of depicting and perhaps had actually taken the bodily presentments of those whose moral power and dauntless courage had left an impression of their appearance, as their teaching and their life had in the words of their opponents, "turned the world upside down." Christians had suffered persecution, the city itself had suffered severely from the Roman Emperor, Septimus Severus, and at the time of Constantine's choice of it, was far below its highest estate. Yet neither Christianity nor art was dead, but both retained sufficient vitality to revive and grow under toleration and encouragement; so when it was made the seat of government, Byzantine artists, inheritors of Greek artistic traditions, were already equipped with the power of drawing and the knowledge of various technical processes to enable them to apply art in the representations of Christian subjects or ideas—whatever of either were required or suitable. At first Christianity neither desired nor required much ornament, and it was at first sparingly used. But the existence of a splendid court and a wealthy and luxurious people, accustomed to appreciating and delighting in all forms of beauty, made the ornamentation and decoration of the sacred writings to increase greatly during three hundred years following the time of Constantine. The basis and ground of the new style was indigenous to the locality, where East met the West, and where Persia, Egypt and Asia Minor contributed ideas and knowledge of art work in metals, mosaics and tissues. Excellence in these and other kinds of art was attracted to the capital of the world to be appreciated, utilized and rewarded. Soon, under the powerful stimulus of exceptional position and circumstances, perhaps more favourable than before or since,

Byzantine artists produced manuscripts in which were decorations made splendid by Greek beauty of form, united to the oriental love and mastery of colour, but mingling with the most solemn truths emblems full of charm and impiety. Gradually, pagan myths, models and phases of thought were introduced, and at the end of three hundred years, all examples in which they appeared were destroyed, and every similar production, for more than one hundred years, considered a crime against the scriptural ideas of earlier times, which were opposed to the worship of images, and saw only sin in the production of either pictures or statues to be used for that purpose. When these extreme opinions were modified, under certain limitations that gradually grew up throughout the eastern empire, art had toleration during the six hundred years that followed, in fact until the last successor of Constantine perished on the walls defending the beautiful capital. Owing to this capture by the Turks, and the action of the iconoclasts, few Byzantine manuscripts remain, especially of the early period, and few in good condition. Yet we know their characteristics, as may be seen on many published examples, are abundant use of gold and colours; figures beautifully drawn and invariably draped; allegory frequently employed, and the representation of suffering avoided. The number of figures in Byzantine manuscripts are generally limited, but the drawing is excellent and, compared with any made at the time elsewhere, shews great superiority; indeed, often where these latter approach excellence it is owing to their being copies or having had Byzantine examples.

The pose and action of Byzantine figures is natural, the drapery graceful, and the drawing correct, so that they possess a certain dignity, and leave an undefinable impression, that they are portraits of actual personages, and that the artists, in representing apostles, prophets and biblical characters, have put before us beings that in form, feature and habit, seem to have lived and moved as they certainly harmonize with what we would expect. It is within the bounds of probability that but for the action of the iconoclasts there would have been evidence making this more of a certainty. These figures are invariably draped, never nude. Christian influence dominating and objecting to the appearance of what was so frequent in Greek art, while the representation of pain or suffering was avoided as it was with the Greeks before them.*

A special characteristic of the style is the abundant use of gold. It was used as a ground on which to write; it was used, in a liquid condition, to write with; it was used as a background to the pictures on manuscripts as a frame surrounding them, as well as to heighten and relieve other colours. These, often very bright, were applied on a ground

---

* The Laocoon is one of the few examples left where suffering is shewn, for in their best period the Greeks considered that the representation of pain and misery was outside the province of art. Professor Gardner in *Sculptured Tombs of Hellas*, says, speaking of monuments to soldiers, "The Greek artists of the good period could not find in defeat and death any elements worthy of their art. They must represent those they portrayed, in the moment of success and victory, not in that of overthrow." And Mýdlleton says "The primitive Christian church avoided scenes representing Christ's death and passion, preferring to suggest them only by means of types and symbols taken from old testament history."

specially prepared to increase the effect, so that a picture on one of their best manuscripts must, in its original condition, have looked like a gold plate on which drawing and writing were enamelled.

Denis says: "The Greek artist painted broadly in a grandiose manner, using thick colours. He began with neutral tints; on them he applied successive shades to mark out the design, which was brought into relief by lights boldly dashed on, and finished by some vigorous touches. The flesh colours ordinarily were very dark, and the brightest tones were kept for the draperies, while the ground was generally gold. The colours employed were of excellent quality, and prepared with extraordinary care, but in many cases insufficient attention has been given to mixing them with suitable substances to make them adhere to the vellum. The varnish or gums employed for the purpose have either been affected by time, temperature, friction, or some other cause, and are reduced to powder, so, becoming detached, have scaled off, carrying the colours with them, and it is painful to read what is said of the ruined condition in which some of them are in Paris." Several manuscripts of the greatest value, they say, cannot be consulted without injury, for scales are ready to fall, as some have already done, leaving part of the picture naked which but for this would, after so many ages, exhibit its original brilliancy. It is not unlikely that the persecution of artists by the iconoclasts had, among other effect, that of destroying the knowledge of various technical processes, and that when toleration was again permitted, materials were used that had not been tested by experience, with a result as unfortunate as with some English artists of this century, when they employed bitumen as a ground to receive their designs.

That the Byzantine artists should use allegory freely was quite consistent with oriental habit and thought, as is seen in the sacred writings, where natural objects are for poetical effect endowed with living action, as, "The sea saw it, and fled"; "the hills skipped like rams." But they went further and, in illustrating Christian writings, gave natural objects human forms, made them deities or genii, with all the attributes of pagan mythology.

There is one Byzantine MS., *Psalmi Davidis et interpretu eorum*, which, being a commentary as well as translation of the Psalms, the painter has tried by figures to make the meaning clearer. In this manuscript there are thirteen pictures of remarkable beauty. Of one, Champollion says: "The desert is shown by a young man, clad in a red mantle, in a seated posture, with outstretched arms. Night is represented by a female figure, erect, in a blue dress, having over her head a veil of the same colour, studded with stars. The Red Sea is a female holding an oar in her left hand, and the depths of the sea is a hideous, swarthy figure, who has seized Pharaoh in his powerful arms, and is dragging him to the bottom." Each of these figures has the name written over it as explanation. This example and others make it certain, to those who have studied the subject, that the Byzantine artists, in attempting to represent the sublime truths, dramatic incidents, or inspired poetry of the sacred writings, while using the resources of Greek art, drew on poetic myths and forms of paganism; and, fine as they might be, and free from immoral suggestion, would be objectionable to those who, strict in interpretation, were guardians of what was orthodox and true. So we can understand their fears, as well as the severity with which they judged all Christian art in which such appeared.

Another peculiarity has been remarked in these manuscripts, which is, that to the reigning emperors and their families was accorded a respect and veneration second only to the deity. Purple was exclusively reserved for their use—for the colour of their robes, the furniture of their sleeping apartments (hence the phrase, "born in the purple"), and the vellum on which their books were written, in letters of gold or silver.

The number of Byzantine manuscripts remaining is comparatively limited. Those before the eighth century may be counted on the fingers. After that period the number is greater. The merest reference to them can here be given. Most writers regarding the style refer to two manuscripts of the fifth century. They were produced after Constantinople was founded, but cannot be considered Byzantine—they were certainly not under Christian influence. One is not a book, but only a number of drawings cut, as the most valuable part, out of a volume of Homer, and the other is a fragment of Virgil. The first is assumed, on good grounds, to be copies of decorations that once covered the walls of some palace or important edifice, and the second to be a poor copy of an earlier Roman work.

The first illuminated manuscript deserving the title of Byzantine, is one at Vienna, on Botany, and was produced for and under the direction of the Greek princess Juliana Anicia. Born in the purple, the grand-daughter of that emperor who was prouder of his accomplishments as a calligrapher than in his possession of a throne—she inherited his tastes and his abilities, which gave her a place as a naturalist and also a painter, though they could not insure her against severe trials, one of which was the assassination of her father, after a very short reign. Another manuscript is in the Vatican, entitled Cosmos Indopleustis, rather later in date, but in style more distinct and perfect, with less of classical manner.

There is also a fragment in the British Museum, of which Shaw, in *Illuminated Ornaments*, gives a facsimile, and says— "It must be considered among the most precious remains of early calligraphy in existence, and formed part of a manuscript that must have belonged to a crowned head, as no meaner individual, at that time, could have been rich enough to cause such a volume to be executed." This fragment is part of two leaves—each of them half of the original size. The ground is gold on both sides. The Greek text, which is the Canons of Eusebius, often attached to the copies of the gospels at that time, is in gold letters within columns and under arches, both of which are formed of various elegant ornaments. The colours are in various shades, mainly of red and blue, the latter from almost white up to deep sapphire. On the arches there are remains of birds and foliage, and in small medallions, busts of the evangelists, which, Shaw remarks, have been "executed in the most masterly style;" which praise is as just as regret is unavoidable at the destruction of much art of which this is an example.

Various others are named and described by writers on the subject as having been executed from the 9th to 12th centuries, which Denis considers was the time within which the most splendid work in the ornamentation of manuscripts appeared. It is thought that very few secular books were decorated by Byzantine artists.

The book most frequently decorated by them seems to have been the gospels, not only for its sacred character which made it become an important part of altar furniture of most cathedrals. And not only was the writing and decoration of the text the finest possible, but the envelope and covering were such as were worthy of an emperor, and in their use by the Bishop, were treated in actual service as worthy of adoration. The number of Greek manuscripts in the British Museum is twenty-one—one of the 6th century, one of the 9th, one of the 10th, the others from the 11th to the 15th centuries. There is one of Genesis, two are of the Psalms, and sixteen are of the Gospels. In Byzantine copies of the gospels there are usually five full-page pictures—Christ in majesty, sitting on a rainbow enthroned. He is surrounded by an oval, and his feet rest on a globe, the symbol of universal power. The other four pictures are of the evangelists, each is either occupied writing his book, or has one in his hand, and is usually represented like an emperor seated on a throne, within an arched canopy, which is supported on Corinthian pillars of marble or other fine stone. In addition to these pictures there are usually decorated pages containing the Canons of Eusebius, which are ten tables where parallel passages of the evangelists are brought together, that they may be more easily compared. In addition, the headings of the books are illuminated, the capital letters being sometimes so large that a few fill an entire page. "These pages are painted over a richly decorated background covered with fluted ornament, and the whole is framed in an elaborate border all glowing with the most brilliant colours and lightened up by burnished gold of the highest decorative beauty." (Middleton).

Byzantine artists in these decorations of the borders seemed to have been less restricted than with figures, for there is more freedom exercised and more variety. The decorations were within ribbon-like forms—leaves and flowers also appear, with birds and animals which are introduced in forms and colour natural or modified as fancy or imagination filled the eye and guided the pencil of the artist—forms both floral and animal are also conventionalized. Denis adds—"They usually are on gold ground, and probably hand down to us souvenirs of an ornamentation, and they are so perfect, that without losing anything of their originality they are in exquisite taste."

What has struck all students of the Byzantine style is

that the figures and mode of producing them is unchanged during eight hundred years. On Mount Athos it is said the monks produce work the same as was done centuries ago, as do the artists in Russia. With them now it is a matter of religion, and time has settled that there should be no change. Yet, beyond that, there seems to be another reason. While Byzantine art, through ecclesiastical considerations of what was proper, crystallized into a form, which to the eyes of the West, accustomed to great variety, is characterized by sameness, even stiffness, yet the Greek artist out of that restriction, or in spite of it, developed an element of dignity which his figures wear, and for certain decorative purposes was and is highly valuable. And so the figures and style that were adopted by Justinian as most suitable to ornament the domes and ceilings of the first Christian temple dedicated to Saint Sophia, the Eternal Wisdom, is found appropriate and effective as ornament to those of St. Paul's Cathedral, in the greater city of London, in the more remarkable reign of Queen Victoria.

Anglo-Saxon.

Water frequently springs up under foot while the fountain head may be hidden, higher up and far away, so the art impulse is often unexpectedly present breaking out apparently from some hidden cause. While the best art of the ancient world was coloured and directed by Christianity, so also was any art that existed in Britain, which, considered among the most barbarous, was also the country most distant from the centre of civilization. While it was natural that the influence of Christianity on art should be seen in the capital, at the fountain head of wealth, power and civilization, it is perhaps strange the next appearance should be at the extremities of the empire, where such were in smallest proportion. A pleasure in beauty which is the touchstone of art, is perhaps first shown by the collection and appropriation of what possesses such, and, when portable, these are kept about the person and become ornaments. Their presence and influence awake the desire and indicate the means for the creation and increase of such, and there is little doubt that ornaments always arose in some such way, and that some kind of them were common through the British Isles before Roman times. We would be justified in believing so, without further evidence, than that no people, as far as we know, have ever existed which had not pleasure in something which, considered beautiful, became ornaments, but the slight reference made by Roman writers, and the remains of incised metals or colored glass, corroborate this, and shew it to have been so in Britain. Whatever power they possessed of ornamental decoration would be applied to anything valued, sacred, or mysterious, including writings. When or by whom Christianity and the books telling of its origin and principles was introduced we do not know, probably it was earlier than generally supposed, and in an apparently accidental way. The ritualism, beliefs, and precepts of Judaism and Christianity, and the difference between them and all other religions in the ancient world, had in many ways been before the Romans, a great number of whom had been present, or seen, or heard, of the events preceding or following the crucifixion, of which the rescue of Paul, and the midnight ride with him to Cæsarea, was only one. And many references, slight in themselves, shew that Roman civilians, such as those of Cæsar's household, military, such as centurions, or of higher rank, had been favourably impressed. The long siege of Jerusalem and its ultimate capture and destruction, and that of its world-famed temple, which Titus vainly tried to save, would all be known throughout the empire, and the subject of conversation or story round the camp fire, wherever a legion was stationed, especially in Britain, where Vespasian and Titus, the commanders at Jerusalem and future emperors, were well known, from having been in authority there, and taken thence soldiers (it is said 20,000), who had assisted at the siege, and seen the destruction of the Holy City. That these events would be early known and of great interest is extremely probable, when we know that in their army natives of widely different parts of the empire—Spaniards, Syrians, and Dacians, from the banks of the Rhine or Vistula,—were quartered side by side on the Roman wall in Northumberland.

If then, merely as events of professional life, some knowledge of Christians or Christianity, however imperfect, found its way into Britain very early by curious or unlooked for channels, such would prepare the way for the labours of those who, impelled by the burning zeal then common, filled the role of the first preachers. It has been assumed the first recognised teachers or preachers came from Spain, which is quite likely.* St. Paul speaks of it as easy of access from Rome, to which it was considered equal in civilization, Vespasian having included it as Latin. It was the native country of Seneca, described as the only great minister under the empire, a contemporary of Paul, and like him a student at Tarsus.

Such a country as Spain once must have been, was sure to be among the first to be visited by Christians, and to receive favourably their teaching. The name of Ireneus is associated with its final acceptance of Christianity, and it is supposed that some of his disciples came in a missionary spirit to Britain and Ireland.

The old name for Spain was Iberne, and for Ireland, Ierne, which might indicate some early connection before Roman times, but whether it was by colonization or conquest matters little.†

The facility of communication before Roman times would be made much easier by their roads, on which one could pass by Watling‡ Street from Dover direct to Chester, where for

* Some think the earliest missionaries were Greek and Eastern, not Latins.

† Fifty years ago in Ireland it was named to me how like people in the south of Ireland are to Spaniards, which has been attributed to some of the Armada settling there, but it may be really owing to much earlier events.

It is curious to know that when the Goths conquered Spain, the civilization they found there conquered them, and that in the 6th and 7th centuries Spain shared with Britain the distinction of being the two countries in Europe where the production of illuminated manuscripts was most successfully carried on— also that a number of Greek artists, leaving Constantinople a century before its destruction, were drawn to Spain, and found more encouragement to go there than either to Italy or France.

‡ The highway between Dover and London existed before the Romans. They paved it and made it a section of what the Saxons afterwards knew as Watling Street—that great road that traverses England from Dover to Chester.

over two hundred years there was a full legion permanently stationed, and by turning westward, from the harbours or creeks of the Mersey, or the Dee, or parts of the Welsh coast, they could pass to Ireland, with which and Wales there was much in common, and had been intercourse long before the Romans were heard of. In fact, communication between the continent and Britain was easier and more frequent than is commonly supposed. Ramsay says, "The organization of that masterful people kept the most distant part of the empire in touch with the central authority, and that the imperial policy fostered intercommunication and unity to the utmost, and it is not too much to say that travelling was not more highly developed, and the dividing power of distance was weaker, under the empire, than at any time before or since, until we come to the present century." The letters of Cicero to his friend in Cæsar's camp in Britain is proof, and there is further confirmation in this, that the 14th legion, comprising 10,000 or 12,000 men, was sent over by Claudius in A.D. 43, it was withdrawn by Nero, sent back again by Vitellius, and finally withdrawn by Vespasian. Many officials, people of importance, came there. Agricola, the governor, spent an entire winter (A.D. 78), at Chester, and also six or seven winters in the north, and in both places, or wherever he was, tried to introduce and shew the advantages of the art and knowledge the Romans possessed.*

* It is even supposed the building of Stonehenge was his act—the object being to Romanise the Britons by blending Roman with Druidic worship—to encourage the chieftains, and find occupation for their sons, to build temples in which they could worship the gods of their fathers, according to a ritual compounded of Roman and other customs.

Even several members of the imperial family visited and stayed in Britain for a time—as the Emperor Hadrian—a native of Spain, who had with him his two sons, Caracalla and Geta. Severus also, who died at York, 208, as did Constantius, the father of Constantine, a hundred years afterwards. These and others would not be there without being accompanied by the wealthy and learned Romans, who in various ways, directly or indirectly, would spread the arts of Greece or Rome over Britain. So when monasteries began to rise, their security and wealth were an aid and protection to all such knowledge as was valued, and it had a better chance of existence and growth in these places, especially the production of the sacred writings and their illuminations, than in Italy itself, subject as it was to internal dissensions and attacks from barbarians. When or where in Britain these manuscripts were first produced, we cannot say, for the few that have escaped the tooth of time, the hand of violence, or ignorance, shew they were produced in Ireland, the north of England, about York, or in the south, mainly about Winchester and Canterbury. Those that remain, as named already, have been classed as Anglo-Saxon, but Sir E. M. Thompson has considered they should be distinguished as Irish, North England, and South England, seeing that, though there is something in common, there is difference enough to need a distinction.

Anglo-Saxon—Irish.

Though the Romans never set foot in Ireland, yet opinion is that the Irish—Scots, as they were called, and called themselves*—derived letters and other signs of civilisation from them; and that, before their time, they were not further advanced — neither better nor worse — than contemporary people in Britain or on the Continent. The illuminated manuscripts produced in Ireland, which are the earliest in Britain we possess, are remarkable for the time, and had an influence, we shall see, outside their native home. Why they were produced there, before elsewhere in Britain, or what were the causes for their cessation, is not for our consideration.† What was characteristic of the style is remarkable still; but when continued in after times, or now, is used as decoration—the accompaniment of art, not art in itself.

As peculiarities of the Byzantine style show what was the art of the ancient Greeks, so does the Irish show us, there is little doubt, what was art among the Scots and Picts—‡

---

* The monastery of St. Gall, in Switzerland, was founded by Killian, an Irish missionary; and, on one of the manuscripts still preserved there, is marked "Scottice Scriptu," written in Irish characters.

† The incursions of the Danes, no doubt, did much injury in Ireland, as they did in England, especially on the Northumberland coast, to various monasteries; but Westwood remarks that "the three centuries that preceded the invasion of Ireland under Henry II tell a fearful tale, and fully prove that Ireland had then, as she has now, greater enemies to her welfare amongst her own offspring than the hated Saxon."

‡ "It is significant that the spiral or whorl, which Westwood particularises as a specially Celtic detail of ornament, is to be seen in the metal-work of shields of British make as early as the first century."—THOMPSON.

simply that of people in an early stage of civilisation, developed to its greatest possible extent under the powerful stimulus of Christianity, through the aid of the security, power, and wealth of the religious communities which Christianity established. Whoever looks at these manuscripts must wonder at the calligraphic skill exhibited, which all writers on the subject highly praise.

Denis speaks of the "rare perfection attained," and says that the scribes "must have had instruments of exceptional delicacy to produce, in their delicate ornamentation, the straight and coiling lines, which the eye only follows with difficulty."

Sir E. M. Thompson speaks of the "marvellous interlaced designs, ribbons and spiral patterns which combine to produce decoration of the highest merit;" and Professor Westwood, who gave much time and thought to the subject, says in his *Paligraphica Sacra:*—"At a time when the fine arts may be said to be almost extinct in Italy and other parts of the continent, a style of art had been established and cultivated in Ireland absolutely distinct from all other parts of the world; that there is abundant evidence to prove that in the sixth and seventh centuries the art of ornamenting the sacred scriptures, especially the gospels, had attained a perfection in Ireland almost marvellous, which, in after ages, was adopted and imitated by continental schools visited by Irish missionaries." He gives the characteristics as "lines straight, curved, coiled, or step-like, interlaced in ribbons or zoomorphic forms, with a profusion of dots, the spiral lines and dots being especially peculiar, and characteristic of the style." In his works he gives representations of the letters X P I— the beginning of St. Matthew's Gospel—from the Book of Kells, and says: "These occupy the entire page, 13 inches by 9¼ inches, and every portion of the letters themselves, as well as the spaces between them, being minutely ornamented and coloured, the whole forming the most elaborate specimen of calligraphy which was probably ever executed." Elsewhere he mentions that he examined one of the drawings of the same book, and counted, on the space of a quarter of an inch, 158 interlacements.*

While unstinted praise is given by these writers when due, not any of them but see deficiencies. Denis says, " The work is rather that of the writer than the painter, all is done with the pen, though heightened with colours, and the principal merit of these calligraphic monuments is in a fineness of execution, a regularity in tracing outlines, which now is only done by engravers' tools."

Thompson says, " The figure drawing is of so primitive and barbarous a nature that it counts for nothing, from the point of view of art;" and Westwood says, "It is indeed a most extraordinary circumstance, that whilst these early manuscripts exhibit a most marvellous perfection in the mechanical treatment of the ornamental details, the higher branches of the art were in the lowest possible state," and

* Twenty years ago, Professor Westwood, in Liverpool, repeated to me personally the substance of these remarks, and, in corroboration, showed me a drawing or copy he had made of one of them, pointing out the marvellous accuracy of the original, and defying me to detect any false or imperfect line.

referring to a drawing of the crucifixion in one of their manuscripts now at Cambridge, says he was unable for a long time to decide what it was intended to represent. "The extraordinary propensity of the Irish schools for marginal rows of red dots, and for twisting everything possible into interlaced and ornamental patterns, the grotesque profiles of the soldiers, the chequered dresses of the figures, create a smile at the poverty of art, which was able only to delineate the most solemn event the world has hitherto witnessed in a manner so liable to be regarded a grotesque. I doubted at first whether the two figures at the sides of the Saviour's head were not intended for the two thieves, but am now able to state they were intended for angels." And of the figures of the Virgin and Child in the Book of Kells, the finest of all Irish manuscripts, he says, "The drawing is entirely puerile, while the ingenuity displayed in the intricate patterns at the sides and upper part of the drawing is quite remarkable." In looking at the representations given it must be admitted there is justification for his remarks. It would seem, then, that the ornaments in Irish manuscripts are chiefly lines of every kind of curve and dots—such seems the beginning of art, both with individuals and nations. Artists invariably work up to what they know, and where gold is not used as color, and there is an absence of figures, or they are badly drawn, art proper has made little progress. Between lines and dots, and the drawing of animals or of the human figure with any accuracy, there is a great distance, and that in Irish manuscripts was never passed.

Gold is profusely used in Byzantine manuscripts as background, and other purposes, but it never is in any way in Irish ones. The metal was found in various places in Ireland, we know from the remains of many personal ornaments, and also because the payment of three ounces of it is mentioned as a payment made, so the reason that it was not used in the illumination of their manuscripts, must have been owing to inability to apply or use it artistically.

North of England.

The long stay of the Romans at York must have had some civilizing influences in the North, and left examples tending to the improvement of any native art then existing, but the beginning of the illumination of manuscripts there is said to be about 635, when Oswald, King of Northumberland, accepted Christianity, and brought an Irish monk from Iona, who founded the Northumberland church, and made Lindisfarne, an island on that coast, the seat of his diocese. Connected with this was a school or scriptorium, from which issued in time a number of finely illuminated works.

The most remarkable of these that remain is one in the British Museum, produced about 700, and known as the Lindisfarne Gospels from the place of origin, Saint Cuthbert's, from being written in honour of that saint; or the Durham Book, from being long preserved in the cathedral of that city.[*]

---

[*] It has an interest through the story told by Sir F. Madden, and all writers who refer to it. The house where it was produced being especially liable to attacks from the pagan sea rovers, the Danes, who respected neither scribes nor

The main features of this manuscript are initial letters, etc., and in them it resembles the best Irish manuscripts. The colours are very beautiful, and laid on so thickly that they produce the effect of enamel or of paintings on porcelain. Gold is also occasionally used, which it never was in Irish manuscripts, and there are four portraits of the Evangelists, of which the drawing is infinitely superior to the barbarism of Irish ones. "These drawings," Middleton says, "instead of being grotesque masses of ornament, like those on Irish manuscripts, are paintings with much beauty of line as well as extreme splendour of colour." They are proved to be but indifferent copies of an example of Byzantine art, brought to England by the Greek Theodore, born at the birthplace of Paul—Tarsus, in Cilicia—who was appointed Archbishop of Canterbury, in 668, and filled the position for fully twenty

scriptoriums, this manuscript was being carried as a special treasure to Ireland, from whence the founders of Lindisfarne came, when in a storm it was carried overboard. Saint Cuthbert, as then believed, was its protector, and took it safely ashore, where a monk of the party, advised in a dream, found it uninjured on the beach, about three miles from where the others had landed. Sir F. Madden says, "The historian, Simeon, records as a miracle that the pages of the manuscript were not in the slightest degree injured by the salt water;" and though there are at present occasional stains on it, yet the illuminations are throughout in the most perfect preservation.

Something similar happened to a manuscript that belonged to Margaret, the Queen of Malcolm Canmore (1056-1093), of Scotland. This, a gospel, was being conveyed some distance that an oath could be taken on the sacred book. The monk who was the bearer, found on his arrival at the appointed place, that it had slipped out of the cloth in which it was enveloped, and was lost. On a careful search, a knight of the suite saw it lying at the bottom of a river, into which it had fallen while being carried across, and which the weight of its metal covering had taken down and kept there; as the leaves were seen waving backwards and forwards by the action of the running stream, it was supposed to be

years. He exercised an important influence for good on his adopted country during his life, and his labours continued to do so after him. Some notice of both cannot be omitted.

Theodore, a Greek, and celebrated as one of the most learned men of his time, owed his appointment to the Greek Emperor of Constantinople, Constans II, whose nominee he was, and whom the Pope Vitalian could not refuse. He appointed him, but under conditions of being accompanied by Hadrian and other decided Romanists. He was acceptable to the British Bishops, the bulk of whom held to the Eastern church, from which their Christianity came, because when it came, there was no other, and though ignorant of English, and over 60 years of age, his religious earnestness, energy, and strength of character, and his complete equipment with the learning and knowledge of the time, made him specially

---

irretrievably injured, hardly worth recovering. But when obtained by diving, it was found the writing was very little injured, and the miniatures of the four evangelists that adorned it not at all. St. Margaret's confessor narrated the incident in poetry, and her joy at the recovery of her treasure, which, especially being uninjured, was by all then considered a miracle. For 800 years the existence of this manuscript and place of deposit was unknown, but about ten years ago, a few books, etc., were sent up from a small church library in Sussex to London to be sold, among them was a manuscript described as of the 14th century. It was sold under that incorrect description for £6, and bought for the Bodleian Library, of Oxford, where its true age, 11th century, was soon determined. An addition made to the text of the manuscript proper, narrated the loss and recovery of it from a river into which it had fallen. A young lady recollected such an incident in the life of a Scottish Queen. With this clue, further research made it evident that here was the long lost manuscript of St. Margaret, and that the small church library at Brent had for long contained something that belonged to, and was treasured by the saint, whose body is now preserved in a chapel built by Philip II of Spain, in the Escurial to contain it as a relic beyond price. Within the last few months, a facsimile of this manuscript has

suitable for his office, which he filled to the entire advantage of the church and state of his adopted country.

It is refreshing to hear with what enthusiasm the old writers, such as Bede, speak of his character and labours, nor are moderns, such as Dean Hook and Bishop Stubbs, much behind. Bede says, "his first care was to visit all the island and teach the right rule of life," and he was the first Archbishop whom all the English churches obeyed. In the schools he founded, he gave instructions, not only in the Book of Holy Writ, but in ecclesiastical poetry, astronomy, arithmetic, music, logic and philosophy, that from him, and others he appointed to preside, there flowed daily rivers of knowledge to water the hearts of the crowds of their hearers. Many of these became noted, and Bede mentions that several were living in his day, as well versed in Greek and Latin tongues as in their own in which they were born, and sums

been issued by W. Forbes Leith, S.J., detailing the circumstances with the mediæval belief in the miracle. From this facsimile it is evident that the miniatures have escaped wonderfully well. I would venture an opinion that, in all cases, the miniatures would suffer less from water than would the writing of the text—mainly owing to what I see has happened to a manuscript of my own, which was exposed to the same mischance. This is a small Book of Hours, written in 1516, and contains twenty small miniatures and twelve larger. It was reached by the water, after a great storm of rain, united with a high tide. The result is that the end leaves are very much stained, indeed, blackened—the writing hardly legible—but the miniatures seem as bright as ever, and are hardly touched. This manuscript belonged to a trader in London, neither better nor worse, as far as I know, than his contemporaries, but certainly unlikely to deserve canonisation or to possess moral qualities that would be insurance against injury to property from heavy rains or high tides. So it seems very likely that the gold, gums, varnish, or something used in the production of the miniatures, has been their protection, and is explanation without seeing it in anything supernatural.

up his life's work—"Nor were there ever happier times since the English came into Britain."

Not the least of the benefits that Theodore conferred were the Greek books he brought, adorned as they were with examples of the best art of the time. They were appreciated and utilised in the monasteries of Northumbria, until their complete destruction by the invading pagan Danes—who seemed to blot them out of existence—as well as in those about Winchester and elsewhere in the south.

SOUTH OF ENGLAND.

Winchester and Canterbury were the chief monastic establishments in the south of England, and it was from them issued most of the best Anglo-Saxon manuscripts. Those that remain indicate the influence, as they recall more or less Irish peculiarities, though gradually, in time, these are less in evidence.

This is apparent in a copy of the gospels produced at Winchester in the 8th century, and presented to York, by Wilfrid, its Bishop, in which was seen, for the first time in England, the Byzantine luxury of purple vellum with a text in gold and silver letters, often used alternately, apparently for the sake of contrast. There is also a Psalter, of the same period, where the initial letters are of the Irish pattern, but the small ones are Roman. It also contains a full page design, which seems but a copy of one in a book brought by Augustine 200 years before. But of all the examples remaining of this school, the most remarkable is the Benedictional, belonging to the Duke of Devonshire, which Westwood considers the noblest example of Anglo-Saxon art, and Ottley says, "The illuminations are among the finest and richest of the period, savouring much of the Greek School." It was made for, and produced under the direction of Athelwold, whose name it bears, a friend of Dunstan, skilled like him in working in metals, who co-operated with him in reforming the monks, refounding and rebuilding churches and abbeys, and in encouraging learning. He was also skilled in music, and delighted in art, of which this manuscript is a proof. He was made Bishop of Winchester in 963, and remained so until his death, in 984. His many good qualities raised him also among the saints, as his disciple, the monk Godeman, who wrote the manuscript, was made Abbot of Thorney.

The following is condensed from the very full description by Gage, in 1832:—

"This manuscript is a folio in vellum of 119 leaves, 11½ inches by 8⅓ inches, and consists of episcopal benedictions for 116 festivals throughout the year. The text is Roman lower case. Anglo-Saxon characters being used in some proper names. The capital initials, some of which are very large, are uniformly of gold. The beginnings and endings of some benedictions, together with the titles, are in gold or red letters—alternate lines in gold, red or black, occur once or twice on the same page—all the chrysographic parts of the Benedictional, as well the miniatures as in the characters in the text, are executed with leaf gold throughout, solid and bright, laid upon size, and afterwards burnished. The book is illuminated with thirty different miniatures, and in addition, thirteen pages highly decorated, some with arches on ornamented columns, or rectangular borders composed of flowers and devices. Each page, where the opening of a principal benediction occurs, being in capital letters of gold, and where a miniature or painting fronts a decorated page, the arches, etc., in both pages are made to correspond. We may add that in this manuscript is introduced what has been remarked as especially characteristic of Byzantine art, the use of allegory, the river Jordan being represented by a recumbent figure with an urn, out of which is flowing floods of water." Gage adds that this manuscript is evidence that there must have been more specimens of art in calligraphy or illuminations in the 10th and 11th centuries executed in this country than in any other, though inclined to think that the works were copied from standard drawings by artists of the Greek school, with which they may have been originally supplied.

We can easily understand that many were produced, if it be accepted as fact what is stated of the number of monks in establishments both in Ireland and Wales. That they were numerous may explain and account for their overflow into countries on the continent. In later examples, such as that called the gospels of King Canute, the acanthus is introduced among the ornaments, with other Roman peculiarities, and also a kind of freehand drawing which seems peculiar to English manuscripts, though perhaps it is only more frequently met with on them than in those of any other nation.

On the whole, the evidence of Westwood, Thompson, Shaw, and most writers on the subject, consider that Anglo-Saxon manuscripts compare favourably with any produced in Western Europe before, and some time after, the Norman conquest. That event doubtless affected architecture, kindred arts, and the ornamentation of manuscripts, and caused any differences to disappear and their approximation to the French, so that, when printing was invented, it was difficult to tell from the mere character of the ornamentation that it was produced in England, and not in France or Flanders.

CARLOVINGIAN.

The manuscripts called Carlovingian come in point of time after Byzantine and Anglo-Saxon. They received the name from Charlemagne, as they were produced in his time, or in that of his immediate successors, through their patronage and aid. They are interesting, not only for their antiquity and the place they occupy in the history of art, but as connected with names constantly met with in the records of the times, and as evidence of an artistic and intellectual movement which made the national life of both France and Germany to seem bright, compared with what preceded or followed—but also to us because the movement was helped, and the measure of success attained was by the aid and employment of British masters. It seems strange to think that from Britain missionaries or teachers should, at that early time, be wanted or able to exercise any influence on the continent. To seek to determine when that began it may be sufficient to mention that, in A.D. 585, about 200 years before Charlemagne, and thirteen years before Augustine came to England, Columkill,* a native of Ireland, went to France, with twelve of his brethren, carrying with him the knowledge he had acquired at Bangor, where, it is said, two thousand were at one time under tuition. He at first founded a monastery at Luxeuil, in France, one in the Rhætian Alps, and another at Bobbio, in Lombardy, where he died, having laboured on the continent thirty years, leaving many precious manuscripts, of which it is said many remain at Bobbio until this day.† Gall, or Gallus, one who came with him, walked in his steps, and founded another monastery in Switzerland, which, called by his name, in after times, attained the supremacy over all other monasteries in Germany, as from it issued both many scholars and manuscripts. The Saxon monk, Wilfrid, Bonifacius, Boniface, as he was called—was a missionary of a later period, whose martyrdom by the pagan Frisians ended in the establishment of Christianity, and his taking the place of the apostle of Germany. But the name most prominent in the Carlovingian movement was he whom the French called Alcuin—he himself signed Alchuine, also Albinus—a native of York, and a member of a noble Saxon

* The French call him Columban, and say he equally belonged to England, France and Italy.

† From its beginning it seems to have been directed by learned and clever men, of whom many are celebrated. Owing to its origin, it was frequently visited by Anglo-Saxons, compatriots of the founder, often bringing gifts of books, sometimes writing them when staying long enough.

family. The tastes of a bibliopole seem to have been born with him: the skill of a scribe, the knowledge of a linguist and a theologian he acquired, and through them the titles then given to certain scholars of "armarius" and "antiquarius." His varied talents and estimable character, less than accident of birth, made him the right hand man of the celebrated Egbert, for thirty-seven years Archbishop of York, and though not in orders was appointed, to the surprise and envy of ecclesiastics who considered one of them only could be qualified for the control and regulation of the library there, which was the largest in Britain or Ireland, and an office of great dignity and importance. In the increase and perfection of it, by obtaining Greek and Latin authors, his zeal and enthusiasm took him wherever there was a chance or hope, especially to Rome, on returning from whence he met Charlemagne, who was interested in the origin and object of his journeyings and labours, and beyond most men could appreciate and correctly value both him and them.* At a second interview, some years afterwards, the favourable impressions on both sides were deepened, various obstacles were removed, the assent of his own sovereign and his spiritual superiors to his residence abroad, with liberty to return, was obtained, and he took service under Charlemagne. It was in A.D. 782, when forty-seven years of age, that he accepted and entered on the duties of master of the palace school which was established in

* Alchuine, speaking of this meeting afterwards, said that what struck him in the Emperor, was his worship of the intellectual life of man, and his innate love of what was beautiful; and wrote to him, "I love in you what you seek in me."

the palace at Aachen, Charlemagne himself and family being among his most attentive scholars.* During eight years he laboriously worked, and in that time he had established a system of calligraphic labours in many of the monasteries of France and Germany, with completely organized "ateliers" at St. Martin du Tours, Aix la Chapelle, Rheims, Orleans, Gall, Metz, and others, and the impulse given, and the light radiating from them, marked an advance which was felt in various parts throughout the empire. It is even thought he founded a school in Paris where the laity might be instructed in calligraphic work, in which the princesses, daughters of Charlemagne, took much interest. If this were the case, it may have been the origin of the lay artists and guilds, by whom so much of the work of the 14th and 15th centuries was afterwards done. In all his labours he wrote to Charlemagne he was cheered by the hope that "through their united efforts they might see in France an Athens, the Athens of Christ, finer than that of Greece." From the various establishments so formed, issued manuscripts, mostly gospels and bibles, of which a number remain, bringing us, as we look at them, into personal relationship with prominent figures of those distant times. It is not always certain that it can be said positively from what scriptorium they issued, or even specify the exact time of production, and the scribe or illuminator is rarely named, but all of them carry on their face some characteristic feature. The movement, we have seen, originated in the commands of the great Emperor. The

* Denis says his title was "Maitre des études en France."

Saxon masters, as artists do now, worked up to what they knew, so their national manner is evident. As their knowledge of figure drawing had been derived from Byzantine examples, that influence is equally present, and the one characteristic is seen in the initials, the other in the figures. As a rule, Saxon is more evident in the earlier works, Byzantine in the later, but in union with national characteristics. In the middle period, there are some in which the Saxon style is very marked, and these are assumed to be the work of Saxon scribes who were only temporarily located in one or other of Alchuine's foundations.

Denis considers that the manuscripts produced in the time of Charles the Bald are what properly deserve the title of being in the Carlovingian style, as they are stamped with an originality which, resting on the foundation of Saxon and Byzantine art, has yet a place of its own. This is very evident in the one called "Gospels of Lothaire," especially in the initials placed profusely at the head of the chapters. In these, the French artists have modified the examples of their Saxon masters by taking away some of their harsh outlines, yet adding to their effect and richness by the use of gold, silver, and other colours varied to admiration. "They have simplified the interlacings, yet preserved the happiest combinations, and, by introducing foliage and symbolical figures, have given an interest and value previously absent." The figures are open to criticism, the accuracy of the Byzantine drawing not being attained, and the rules of design being greatly outraged, yet "they have a certain nobleness of attitude, and for the most part an austere gravity of expression, which evidence a deep feeling of reverence and devotion."

A good many Carlovingian manuscripts exist, most of them in various public libraries in France. They have been described, and examples of their illuminations given, in various works, which those interested can consult. Only two or three can be here referred to.

One of the most celebrated is what is called the "Hours of Charlemagne," though it properly is an Evangelarium, being a selection of 242 lessons from the gospels, arranged for use during an entire year. It occupied a scribe named Godeschah seven years, and is written in round (uncial) letters of gold, upon purple vellum, and has six miniatures. Like most of these manuscripts it has had many owners, and escaped various dangers, as did those of St. Cuthbert and St. Margaret. It was long in an abbey at Toulouse, but in 1793 was dragged thence, and stripped of the metallic binding which had protected it for 900 years. It was then thrown, naked, with many more, in a heap destined to be sold as waste. While in that evil case it was accidentally seen by one who could appreciate its value, and his efforts at rescue, fortunately, were successful in getting it a place in the city library, where it remained for nearly twenty years, and only passed thence, as the noblest present the city could offer, to Napoleon I, on the birth of his son the King of Rome. It was received joyfully, and became the greatest treasure in the rich collection at the Louvre, which Napoleon reserved for his own use, and daily consulted,* and narrowly escaped destruction during the late siege of Paris by the Prussians.

The Bible of Alchuine, another of these manuscripts, is an amended version of the translation of Jerome, which, having become corrupt, was undertaken by order of Charlemagne. This copy was produced under Alchuine's own eye, in the celebrated abbey of Martin du Tours,† to which he was appointed abbot in 796, and where he died in 804, and was buried. It was destined as a present to Charlemagne on his coronation at Rome on the 25th December, A.D. 800, which was then reckoned the new year's day of 801. He sent it by the hands of his countryman and favourite pupil, Nathaniel—whose real name was Fridugis—who succeeded him as abbot, and became afterwards chancellor to Louis Debonair. In the letter that accompanied the gift he said: "After deliberating long time what the devotion of my mind might find worthy of a present equal to the splendour of your imperial dignity, at length, by the inspiration of the Holy Spirit, I found what it would be competent for me to offer, and fitting for your

* No doubt this would be of great interest to Napoleon, for he was pleased to class himself with Alexander, Cæsar, and Charlemagne, whose place he had reached, and whose power he was exercising. We never can tell what influence the acts of those conquerers had in the schemes formed by that wonderful brain. If Alexander's career directed his thoughts towards Egypt and India—or Cæsar's towards Britain—it was an Englishman, who at St Jean d'Acre, barred his way to the one, as it was another who prevented him or any of his army ever setting foot on its shore, excepting as a prisoner. "Nelson's far distant storm beaten ships, upon which the grand army never looked, stood between it and the dominion of the world."—*Mahan*.

† In it was founded a school, where the liberal arts were taught with such success as to produce, in the succeeding century, the most celebrated scholars of Europe.

prudence to accept. For nothing appeared more worthy of your peaceful honour than the gifts of the Holy Scriptures, which, by the dictation of the Holy Spirit and mediation of Christ God, are written by the pen of celestial grace for the salvation of mankind." This volume is a large folio, 20 inches by 14¾ inches. Consisting of 449 leaves of extremely fine vellum, it is written in 50 lines to the page, in a minuscule character, in double columns of 15 inches high, 4¾ inches broad. It begins with the title to Jerome's Epistle to Paulinus, written in capital letters of gold nearly an inch in height, on bands of purple, which are enclosed in a border surrounding the entire page, composed of gold intertwined ornaments within an edge of green or gold, with eight larger, and an equal number of smaller, interlaced ornaments in silver. It has four large miniatures, the first (divided into four compartments), containing representations of the creation of Adam and Eve, Eve presented to Adam, the Temptation, and the Expulsion. The next is at the beginning of Exodus, and is divided into two compartments—Moses receiving the Law, and Moses expounding the Law. At the beginning of the New Testament are the Canons of Eusebius. Then follows an illumination occupying the entire page. In it is represented the Saviour (whose features are young and beardless) seated on a globe, with a nimbus round the head, the right hand being raised in the act of benediction, and the left holding a book. At the end of the volume is the fourth illumination, divided into two parts, and illustrative of the Apocalypse. After

Charlemagne's death, it is not known where this manuscript was disposed, but when, in 1793, the French troops invaded Switzerland, it was sold, and remained in private hands for nearly fifty years, until obtained in 1836, for £750,* by the British Museum, and no more appropriate resting-place could be found for this work of the most learned Anglo-Saxon, perhaps, in Europe of the time, who was an honour to the country of his birth, as he was a benefit to that of his adoption and the entire world, nor, possibly, if he had a choice, was there any place where he would have been more desirous it should rest. It would, doubtless, have been a pleasant thought to him if he could have realised what would be the position of that country at the end of a thousand years, and his intensely human nature would have had great satisfaction in seeing not only the material power and influence it exercised, but the intellectual life evident all around, to which his work and labour had contributed. For, in expatriating himself from worthy motives, he never lost an affection for his native land, and retained always the right of returning— which he did for a year or two—and always cherished the hope that his bones would rest there, and though that was not to be, yet at the last he pleased himself to think that his spirit would be again in the cloisters of York Minster as in youth, while the brethren sang their vespers, and that

* This is only about a tenth of what was first asked. Sir T. Madden, in the *Gentleman's Magazine*, gives an account of the efforts of the vendor to make a good sale, as well as of the manuscript itself and all that is known of its real history. Professor Westwood, in *Paligraphia Sacra*, also does the same, with some coloured examples of the illuminations.

his soul would pass upwards with the last cadence of their praise.*

The Bible of Charles the Bald is another celebrated Carlovingian manuscript which, if not so interesting from associations as the last two, is superior in point of art, containing as it does more distinctive national characteristics. It was produced in the same abbey as the last, about fifty years later, and for the same object, as a gift, this time to the grandson of Charlemagne, Charles the Bald, King of France, to whom, doubtless, it was very acceptable, as he was even a greater lover of what was beautiful than his grandfather. This was doubtless much owing to his mother, the accomplished Judith, under whom his natural inclinations were guided and encouraged, so that, though the liking for illuminated manuscripts was marked in many of the children and grandchildren of Charlemagne, judging from what is said and from what remains, he exceeded them all. Some accounts say that he and his sister Ada caused many copies of the Gospels to be written in gold. This Bible was the result of the labours of Count Vivien, the abbot, and the scribes of the abbey, and the presentation is shown in one of the miniatures of the book—interesting as evidence of the ideas of the time of the value then given

---

* He wrote: " My fathers and brethren, dearer than all else in the world,—pray don't forget me, for alike in life and death I shall ever be yours. And peradventure God in mercy may grant that you that nursed my infancy may bury me in old age. But if some other place be appointed for my body, yet I believe my soul will be granted repose among you through your holy intercession and prayers."

to such gifts, as it would for ever be the title-deeds of ownership. Charles, in his royal robes, is regally seated in full court, while the abbot is accompanied by his monks. The volume is a folio, 20 inches by 15 inches, written in a Carlovingian minuscule, the commencement of each book being in golden letters on a purple ground. The initials are of very large size, some as much as 10 inches, and highly ornamented, and are frequently accompanied by symbolical figures by which the artist has sought to make the text clearer. In the letter D, in one case, are the twelve signs of the Zodiac. Westwood says: "The framework of many of the pages is elaborately ornamented with Arabesques of great beauty, and even of Grecian purity," and Denis says these "only yield in value to the initials."

The volume also contains seven illuminations of great beauty, approaching in general design those in Alchuine's Bible—produced in the same abbey fifty years before—but a higher degree of technical skill being evident.

The "Hours of Charles the Bald" is the last to be mentioned. It is decided to have been written between A.D. 842 and 869, but not known where, by one Luithard, whose nationality is not known nor determinable by the style, which differs from all others produced for Charles the Bald. It is entirely in uncial letters of gold. The titles are in gold on bands of purple; the initials are within frames of large size, filling an entire page, and executed in the purest taste. Denis says: "In these there is evidence of an effort to attain perfection which has succeeded; all that the imagination could dream the hand has realised, and elegance is united with dignity." The manuscript contains three miniatures, which are the best of their time, though, as in all of that age, the design and drawing are not faultless.

Subsequent to A.D. 1000.

It has been already noted that in France the beginning of art proper was practically in the illuminations of manuscripts, and was initiated by Alchuine, and made possible by the aid and support of Charlemagne, and of his immediate successors. How much was owing to them is seen in this, that when that patronage and aid ceased, after the death of Charles the Bald, art in France began to decline, and before the dawn of the 11th century had entirely disappeared.

The schools or educational system, however, established by them in various parts of the country, continued to exist and bear fruit long afterwards. The tenth century in France was very unfavourable to any advance in art or learning, and closed in darkness and depression, owing greatly to the idea, widely prevalent there, that A.D. 1000 was the period indicated by prophecy as the termination of the 'world. One of their writers on the subject says " The clergy preached it, and people had other things to do than to ornament books;" and Hallam says " Many Charters began with the words 'as the world is now drawing to a close, etc.,' and an army under Otho I was so terrified by an eclipse of the sun, which they took to be a sign of the end, that they dispersed on all sides."

That other part of Charlemagne's kingdom, Germany, was

not affected to the same extent. Christianity was preached and accepted at Metz, A.D. 340—150 years before Clovis, king of France, was baptised. Communication between Germany and the east was closer and more frequent, and thousands of articles, the production of a higher civilization, found their way there, so art had a footing, and an existence, before the time of Charlemagne, and though helped by him was not created by him, as it was in France. So when, after his death, France was suffering from political troubles, the incursions of the Normans, and paralyzed under the terror of gloomy anticipations, art was vigorous in Germany, partly from the prevalence of comparative peace, the encouragement of its sovereigns, particularly Lothaire, Charlemagne's grandson, the increase of wealth through commerce with the east and Constantinople, which supplied Byzantine models and pictures for teaching and imitation. The influence of Byzantine art, then at its best, is seen on that of Germany, by manuscripts now existing in the libraries of Brussels, Munich, etc., which, produced at that time, are equal to the best Carlovingian work of France. When, however, the dreaded time had passed harmlessly, nations breathed more freely, and the opening of the 11th century seemed the breaking of a day of good hope for all, especially for France. Contributing to this was the settling of nations within more defined boundaries, the increase of population, the growth of laws and customs, founded on, or modified by, Christian principles, which, imperfectly as they were understood or practised, or realized, were in regard to human life, infinitely superior to the civilization of the Roman Empire, or the savage paganism of the northern hordes, that had swept it away and taken its place. Concurrently with these changes, partly emanating from them, there was the decline of the feudal system, the increased importance of civil communities, the power and wealth of the church, which, from its constitution and the Orders in it, was, on the whole, favourable to the practice and production of art; monastic bodies being fitted and well able to give it security and aid, which they did, especially when helping or not opposed to their objects. The Crusades, also, the sentiments, the heroism, even the ignorance which initiated the movements, caused the efforts and entailed the losses, had an awakening and stimulating effect on Europe. Arising out of the Crusades, to provide means for them, much landed property changed hands, privileges were acquired, traffic increased, travel followed, and thousands perished, yet bringing, in the train of all these, new ideas, and generally an increase of knowledge. A noticeable effect as connected with art, was a love of brilliancy and splendour, both in public and private life, as described in chronicles or shown by illuminations. In these, new subjects are treated, strange and novel figures are introduced, brighter colours are employed, and in all kinds of art there is less of hardness and more of flexibility and grace than formerly. Architecture was influenced, even writing was modified, and its lines became more flowing and less rigid. As was natural with these changes, there was increased liking for books, and desire for their acquisition,

Styles of Illumination subsequent to A.D. 1000.

signs both of increased wealth and more learning. The craving was not only for books of theology, but for those about other countries, times or events, history, poetry, and romance—so while books increased, so did illuminations and ornamentation.

The demand, monastic scriptorums could not, often would not, supply. Consequently the number of lay professors of every kind, scribes, decorators, and miniaturists greatly increased from the 12th century onwards. The result, as to be expected, was changes in the patterns and forms of decoration.

The drawing, both of inanimate forms or of living and moving figures, became more accurate, and drapery and other accessories were according to contemporary costumes. The single figure was increased to be a group, and made to fill part or the whole of a page. They were also inserted in the initial letters as well as the borders, and the margins of books assumed proportions to the text, and to each other. Whether margins were first adopted for the purpose of ornamentation need not be considered, they certainly were utilized for that object, and, where cost was not a question, were fully occupied. The subjects on them gradually took a wider range—plant forms were not limited to ivy and wild geranium, but included leaves of various kinds, and most of the best known flowers, pink, daisy, violet, strawberry, etc. These and many other kinds of decorations were applied, especially to Books of Hours, and also for several centuries to most documents of importance.

Among others, there were rolls peculiar to monasteries or religious foundations, containing obituary notices of patrons and members. These rolls, which are rarely seen, passed from one establishment to another, claiming the prayers of the brethren for the souls of the departed members or benefactors. Tite says "The colours on these must have been brilliant beyond measure, as on the few that remain, notwithstanding the many thousand times they have been unrolled, vividness and beauty still shine." But religious ceremonies, state receptions, scenes of domestic and peaceful life, the brilliant tournament or war, its pomp and circumstances, or its stern reality, were all represented. Such were not only of interest and delight, but were accepted as proof and confirmation of the event, and no doubt they were frequently given for the purpose of sealing the truth of what was narrated, just as a photograph is very often now. I have an Italian manuscript, a "Matricola" or book of the rules, minutes, and proceedings of the society of St. Nicholas, in Venice, from 1550 onwards. In it are recorded several law suits in which the society was involved. The circumstance is not only stated, and the decision of the court given, but there is a representation of the scene. The judges are on the bench, the parties are pleading, etc. Pictures of saints, performing the miracles associated with them were often given[*] and the abundance of saints and and miracles had much to do with the adoption and retention

---

[*] In the *Times* of May 28, 1897, there is described the Canonization in Rome of two priests, among other things done, it says, "Pictures of miracles performed by the intercession of the two saints were hung round the dome."

of ordeal of battle, and also in forming the opinion so universal in the middle ages, that in such a contest, God would shew and did "defend the right."

It would be out of place in this sketch to attempt to describe or give details of the changes or variations that may have taken place in the decorations of manuscripts in the chief countries of Europe from the 11th century onwards, or to note the ebb and flow as the art suffered, as it did in all of them, during wars, epidemics or famines, or flourished in peaceful and prosperous times, or through the aid of enlightened rulers or wealthy amateurs, so only some salient points regarding our own country or our neighbours are here referred to.

As long as Constantinople remained in Christian hands, which was up to 1453, Byzantine artists produced more or less good examples of their own style, which, as named, was essentially Greek art, within traditional or ecclesiastical limits; but when the last emperor died on the walls of his capital, and his empire passed to the Turks, the artists who could escape, finding themselves and their art out of place there, naturally directed their course to Italy.

In Italy, for centuries before this time, mainly owing to the great unrest there, arising chiefly from the efforts of the Popes to obtain political power—which they seemed to use unwisely when obtained,—art was at a very low ebb; in the thirteenth century much below either France or England. But in the next century there was a marked revival, among other things the great wealth and power of the

Papacy;* a personal liking by some of the Popes for art; the increasing use of it in the service of the church; the wealth that, through commerce and the Crusades, had come to the trading communities of Venice, Genoa, Pisa, etc. These were among the reasons why, in the fifteenth century, art in Italy attained a high degree of excellence, and in the illumination of manuscripts was superior to all other nationalities. In the middle of that century Greek artists from Constantinople brought there their knowledge and technical skill, and in the various art centres of Florence, Parma, Sienna, and others, found a patronage for their talents, and a wider field for their exercise, one free and unhedged by Byzantine restrictions, so that in the sixteenth century Italy was, in every form of art, without a rival.

In looking at the miniatures and illuminations on some of the manuscripts then produced, in regard to the variety of forms, their arrangement and combination, or the beauty, delicacy, and harmony of the colours employed, and the grace and elegance over all, it is difficult to imagine anything finer, or nearer perfection. Representations of imagined forms, natural or conventional, in the animal or vegetable world, are in great variety, as well as coins, medals, and precious stones uncut or sculptured; while the colours almost look, in their richness, as if ruby, sapphire, emerald, or peritot had been dissolved, and applied in a liquid condition. Middleton says

* In the sixteenth century the tax payable yearly to the Pope by Canterbury was 10,000 ducats. Treves, Coblentz, and Mayence were rated the same, which would be equal to £20,000 of our money.

"In some cases their technical qualities bear witness to an almost superhuman amount of dexterity and patience," and that "words are inadequate to describe the refined beauty of the best Italian manuscripts." Such, as should be expected, were never abundant, and are now very rare, being found or seen only in national or in a few private collections. Most Italian Books of Hours offered for sale are smaller in size than French ones. The miniatures are fewer, and only around them, rarely round the text, is there an illuminated border. One kind is a ground formed of narrow gold lines, like worm-marks, among which are interspersed small conventional forms, and also medallions on which are deer, hares, birds, or monkeys in a landscape. This style is considered as having been specially the productions of artists at Sienna. Another form of border is a ground of blue, ruby or gold colour, over which run conventional or natural floral lines, in contrasted colours, carrying small medallions containing saints, angels, and amorini. Another kind of border has rather an eastern appearance, and was used up to a late period, being often applied to the first page, forming a decoration of the earliest books printed in Italy.

The peculiarity of this decoration is that, starting from the bottom, running along it and up the outer and inner borders, are gracefully-twining branches, the outlines of which are gold, but the stems are white, and among the convolutions, birds, insects, and flowers are occasionally introduced, the spaces between being filled in with gold or bright colours. In some of the finest late Italian manuscripts, produced for

Popes or high dignitaries of the church, classical ornaments, such as were adopted in the decoration of apartments in the Vatican and other places by Raphael and his school, are introduced in rich profusion. The Popes and others continued, long after printing was invented, to have books copied and decorated for them, and the republic of Venice, also, to decorate their Ducale. These were credentials given by the Doge to governors or other officials. They were often a volume of two hundred leaves, and contained the appointment and instructions, or the laws to be administered, with the portrait of the official, and some other decorations, by one of the many artists that abounded there; Titian and Paul Veronese being among those believed to have worked on such. Whoever they were by, they were often of great beauty, for which reason they seldom remain in the volume to which they belonged.

FRANCE.

As to France, one of their own writers says: "The 11th century has left us few examples, and those are extremely barbarous, sentiment of beauty or power of design being very distant." In the 12th century the decadence is arrested and a new and better influence is apparent. In the 13th the Gothic is entirely dominant, and is perceptible in the form and colour of everything, including writing and architecture. This is the time of the Crusades and of St. Louis IX, who was contemporary with our Henry III, and, like him, a lover of books and art. Both monarchs had an influence in their respective countries, and at that time there was little difference in the character of the art current in both. The beginning of the 14th century was the time when what was called the ivy leaf pattern of border, with diaper background to miniatures, began. It was universally used there for fully a century, to be modified by the introduction of acanthus leaf, or some other natural or conventional form, and was followed by the adoption of architectural compositions as borders, or as frames for miniatures, in which gold was much used, by shading, to bring into relief the tracery of shafts, arches, canopies, etc. From 1450 and for some time afterwards, the margins or borders were often in mathematical divisions, circles, squares, diamonds, heart or other shapes, having gold or other coloured grounds, on which were painted foliage, flowers, fruit, or figures, the latter often fantastic and unnatural. Both the ground and devices on them were made as agreeable as possible by the contrast of colours. In some, also, both French and Flemish, knotted cords or cables bearing mottoes, with brown backgrounds, and shades of lilac, green, blue, or gold with flowers or insects, or both, represented on them. In books of alchemy—not very abundant—borders of dead gold, on which birds, flowers, butterflies, and insects seem preferred, as if the belief in the transmutation of metals was only in accordance with changes in insect and vegetable life. Later, medals, precious stones, and pearls are represented, united with classical ornaments.

Until the invention of printing there was continual progress, and a general appreciation, arising much from the liberal encouragement of sovereigns and great feudatories of France, which caused the production of much art of the highest excellence in illuminated manuscripts. Much was done by laymen, working singly, or in co-operation as members of guilds, for the general public, or under the patronage or in the actual service of a long series of French kings and semi-sovereigns of Flanders, of princes, nobles, or rich commoners.

Mainly from these guilds in France and Flanders (Bruges, Antwerp, and Brussels especially), issued an immense number of *Horæ*, which were produced more cheaply and rapidly than hitherto. Partly owing to this, and partly owing to the greater destruction in some other countries, at the Reformation, it happens that in all public and private collections of illuminated Books of Hours the proportion of French and Flemish to others is at least five to one.

English.

The number of English manuscripts is comparatively small, and they are mainly in various national collections where only they can be studied and comparisons made with those of other nationalities. There are enough of them to establish that the superiority that gave masters to France, in the 8th and 9th centuries, was maintained through the 10th and well into the 13th century, and that manuscripts produced within that time compare favourably with any produced elsewhere. The French author who described those of his country in the 11th century as "barbarous," says "those of the Anglo-Saxons then were beautiful enough." One of our own writers, Middleton, speaks' very decidedly, and says, "In the 10th century, the Winchester school of illumination appears for a while, at least, to have been the foremost of the world. Both in delicacy of touch and in richness of decorative effect, the productions of this school are superior to those of any contemporary continental country. In the 11th century, miniatures showed beauty of form and gracefulness of pose—in the 12th rapid advances were made towards perfection, both in design and technique, and extremely fine miniatures were produced. The culmination was in the 13th century, which, for beauty of all kinds, remained for a long time quite without a rival in any European country, and, for a brief period, England occupied the foremost position in the world with regard to nearly all the principal branches of the fine arts. "There is, in short, ample evidence to show that the Anglo-Norman art of the 13th century in almost all branches, more especially on English soil, had reached a higher pitch of perfection, æsthetic and technical, than had been attained by any other country in the world." In the 14th and 15th centuries, owing largely to the black death and the Wars of the Roses, the arts of England fell into the background. From A.D. 1400 onwards, the illumination of manuscripts in England gradually ceased, and continental styles were adopted. When any illuminated manuscripts, after that time, were required they were obtained from France or Flanders.* The artists of those countries were numerous

* In the British Museum is an illuminated manuscript, entitled, "*Histoire Scholastique, contenant du luivre de Thobie jusqua les Fais des Apôtres—Le quel Luivre fut fait à Bruges par le Commandement de Roy Edouard IV, l'an 1470, escript par J. du Ries.*"—BRADLEY.

and skilful enough to supply them cheaper and more expeditiously than could be done at home; and, when Books of Hours or other illuminated manuscripts ceased to be wanted, but pictures of events or portraits of people were, Holbein, Vandyke, Rubens, and others took up the pencil that had fallen from the hands of the old illuminators, and continued to supply the kings and nobles of Britain with new forms of art. From this it will be seen, that, in the 13th century English miniaturists held the first place, in the 14th it was the French, and in the 15th and 16th it was the Italian.

De Gray Birch in his valuable work* indicates with accuracy and truth differences, in manner and style, in the illuminations of different nationalities. He says: "The English are famous for clearness and breadth; the French for delicate fineness and harmoniously assorted colours, the Flemish for its minutely stippled details, and the Italian for the gorgeous yet calm dignity apparent in the best manuscripts. In the French style of art we find brightness and grace of colouring, with wonderful delicacy of detail, especially in the faces, which often have a beauty of expression, astonishing when we consider the very limited space occupied. The Flemish are remarkable for the great excellence of their delineation of natural objects and of buildings, and this excellence to have culminated in their beautiful landscapes and interiors. To the bright and harmonious colouring of the French the Italian adds warmth and richness. The landscapes of the Flemish school are not more true to nature and pleasing to

* *Early Drawings and Illuminations*, by W. De Gray Birch and Henry Jenner.

the eye than those of Italian artists. In the delineation of the human form, Italy is not inferior to the other two; and in the treatment of limbs and muscles, a knowledge of anatomy and modelling is shown that is unknown to French and Flemish illuminations."

That there are the differences just noted in the treatment of the same class of subjects, by different nations, must be owing to national peculiarities, which the illumination of manuscripts did not create but only made evident; so neither would those differences cease with them, but appear in any new phase of art and be seen in some different form. After the invention of printing painting on a larger scale, on panel or canvas, took the place very much of that on manuscripts. On looking on many Italian paintings the miniaturists seem still working on different materials, and many figures, both before and after Perugini and Raphael, recall, if they are not actually modified or reclothed, forms of those that had appeared in manuscripts; while the peculiarities of the landscapes in the Flemish Hours of the 15th century, noted by Birch, appear a century afterwards in Flemish cabinet pictures of Ruysdael, Hobbema, Cuyp, and others. Differences were also apparent in the illuminations in French and English Books of Hours, as there is now, not only in their art productions but in their mode of accepting or dealing with most incidents. The beautiful pageants and feverish excitement we hear of in the French capital, even in that lately given and exhibited on the recent visit of the Czar of Russia, seem but a variation and repetition of some described by Froissart, and which was so different and such a contrast to the behaviour of the people in England on similar occasions, that in describing some he saw there, Froissart used the phrase, "the English take their pleasures sadly." An English chronicler of that time very likely would have been disposed to say of the French, that in their excitement their pleasures are taken madly.

To-day, in the excellence of their designs and beauty of their modelling, the French exhibit the superiority noted in their illuminated manuscripts of five or six hundred years ago, and the frequent representation of the nude in their pictures now, or the questionable morality of their novels and plays, is not anything new. It is not the outcome of the Revolution, nor the production of atheism or republicanism, but was apparent not only in many of the romances and chronicles but in the illuminations in their Books of Hours, and other religious books.

Langlois, in his *Essay on Calligraphy*, quotes Henry Etienne, who says: "Ceci puis je asseurer que j'ai livres en parchemin contenons matins, vespres, complies, et les autres pieces de tel service esquels en certains endroits sont peintes des jeunes dames qui ont un maintien lascif." From his own knowledge he gives instances, adding: "Nous ne pouvons néanmoins dispenser de l'avouer ces vieux *enlumineùrs*, etrangers pour la plupart aux moindres régles de la décence et de la pudeur, se permirent souvent des licences dont n'approchaient qu' á peine celles des *fabloyeurs* leurs contemporains, dans leurs scandaleux recits." While Langlois speaks from full knowledge, yet neither in the many French Books of Hours in private collections or offered for sale have I seen corroboration—possibly because examples in which they were would not be readily saleable in England. Of some English manuscripts there may be some illustrations, and may have been more in those destroyed not over delicate, but not anything could be said of them such as this Frenchman says of those of his country; while in English illuminations there is evidence of a sense of humour,* and an enjoyment of it, which our artists and writers have ever possessed and exercised. This is what Waagen says the illuminations of English manuscripts tell.

Speaking of a Psalter of the date 1160-80, he says: "Many subjects are conceived in a style that occurs in no miniatures of contemporary period, while the realistic tendency so native to England is seen in every circumstance—the work abounds with initials of great elegance, and with decorations of the lightest and most refined character." Of another, about 1250: "This exhibits earnest religious feeling with the most unrestrained humour. For instance, on one page there is an ass playing the lute, a monkey the violin, a baboon being behind with a squirrel on a chain; a monster

* A curious instance is seen recently in the remark of the younger Brunet, who, though a countryman of Moliere, speaking of Frognall Dibdin, says: "This humour is peculiar to our neighbours, and is a special production of the soil of Britain. We neither possess the thing nor a word describing it, and all imitations have invariably been unsuccessful. We are, however, so rich in other qualities that we get on very well without it ("Nous sommes d'ailleurs assez riches pour nous passer de cette quality"). This union of critical insight and genuine self-complacency, if not humour, serves the purpose.

playing an unknown instrument, a hare striking the cymbals, a pig blowing the Pan's pipe, a monkey playing the guitar, and a ram the violin. Such strange combinations, at so early a period, are not exhibited, that I am aware of, by the miniatures of any other nation."

Of another, about 1320, he writes: "This manuscript illustrates the high cultivation and great originality of the English school of the time, nor am I acquainted with any miniatures, either Netherlandish, German, or French, of this time which can compare in artistic value with the pictures executed by the best hand in this manuscript. Animals are represented with much truth to nature, and even horses are incomparably better than in many otherwise excellent miniatures of the period. There is, besides events from sacred and profane history, a number of humorous subjects, which are among the cleverest and most original specimens of the kind that have descended to us from the Middle Ages, proving that this master possessed all the characteristic qualities of English art—the realistic, and the fantastic, and the humorous in an unusual degree." And of the period from 1300 to 1360: "The English miniatures agree in the chief features with those of France and the Netherlands. Instead, however, of the gaudy and sometimes unbroken colours, blue and vermilion, seen in the French and Netherlandish schools, the English miniaturists retained the less bright colours of the 13th century, which are even harmoniously broken with lighter tints. In the larger initials, figurative subjects are gradually introduced for mechanical flourishes. The small initials are of burnished gold on a ground of body colour, blue or brown, the use of rose colour is remarkable in the decoration of the border, and the clean and precise execution is worthy of admiration. Animals exhibit great truth to nature. As regards the moral elements of a picture, the fantastic and the allegorical are no less conspicuous than in manuscripts of other countries, but the inventions of the English in this line are very original, while they develop the allegory of the two trees—the one bearing virtues and the other vices—more fully than any other nation."

From these and other extracts that might be given, it is evident that this intelligent foreigner placed the English miniaturists high in the possession of every artistic quality, and seems to have been especially struck with the sense of humour and originality, and also, indirectly, by characteristics in life, art, and literature present ever since. And that they existed six hundred years ago and exist now, cannot be considered a mere freak or accidental circumstance. If they have not been apparent or been in abeyance during centuries, that has been owing to circumstances. The plague and the wars of the Roses at one time, the wars of the Commonwealth and religious fermentation at another, foreign wars, the attractions of adventure, sport, commerce, politics, and other things, all had influence in turning the thoughts and directing the energies of Englishmen in these directions rather than in that of art, as was done by some nations on the Continent. But when the abilities and tendencies of our countrymen have had free scope, a host of names comes up. Hogarth, Reynolds, Gainsborough, Cruikshank, Wilkie, Landseer, Scott, and Dickens have shown themselves lineal descendants and worthy successors of the unknown illuminators to whom Waagen gives such honour.

S. R. Gardiner, in his "*Cromwell's Place in History*," says, "It is beginning to be realized that whatever may be the opinion of some of Cromwell's isolated actions, he stands forth as the typical Englishman of the modern world. To some he is the champion of liberty and powerful progress, to another the forcible crusher of free institutions, to a third the defender of oppressed people, to a fourth the asserter of his country's rights to dominion. Each has something on which to base his conclusions. What is more remarkable is that this union of apparently contradictory forces is precisely that which is to be found in the English people, and which has made England what she is." As the English people of to-day are seen in the individual Cromwell of two hundred years ago, and also many of their characteristics in the miniatures of manuscripts of four or five hundred years before Cromwell, it is not surprising to find indications that the qualities in evidence at such different times and in such different ways should also have existed, though latent and unobserved, eighteen hundred years ago when the Romans came. We know that they considered the Britons to be physically a superior race—indeed, spoke of them as being giants, and were struck with the fine dogs and horses they possessed—they also found the women were more on an equality with men than in other barbarous people they had met on their conquering career. Climatic peculiarities were favourable for all these—perhaps the chief cause of their existence; and, as they have never since ceased working in the same direction, so there is reason the qualities then existing should continue. The agreeable temperature throughout the year is tempting to out-door life, exercise and occupation, equally for both sexes. Twice a day the sea is ever visiting our shores, running far inland, carrying healthful breezes. The prevalent moisture gives fertility to the soil, brightness to the verdure, and clearness and beauty of complexion to the inhabitants—which was noted at St. Augustine's time and since. The existence of good horses and dogs in Britain at the very earliest period of our history, trifling as it may seem, is a singular instance of the permanence of national characteristics. It is a sign that Britons were fond of them, and that they were well treated, and anyone must recognise how marked a feature that is with Englishmen all the world over in the present day. Nowhere, and by none, are horses and dogs better or more valued, and so often treated as companions and friends than in England and by Englishmen; and nowhere else is there such a consensus of opinion that humanity to them is a matter of course duty, and made legally enforceable.

The equality of the sexes, which was greater in Britain in Roman times than elsewhere, is a striking feature. It has ever been maintained, and, ever acting, has ever been an advantage. In 1328 a law was passed in France " that it was too great a country to be ruled by a woman," yet a century had hardly passed before it was delivered from foreign domination by one—Joan d'Arc; and it was France, of all countries, that gave adoration to a woman as the "goddess of reason." England has not gone to either of these extremes, for, so far as I know, there has never been a time in its long and chequered history when the hardest heads in it have refused any duty or service, merely because it was from a woman the order came. Indeed, it is strange to see at the very beginning of our national history a queen, Boadicea stands out possessing some of the national qualities (so far as comparison can be made) marked in Cromwell*—fearless, and like him, cheerfully obeyed to the death; while at the present time it is again a queen, who, in greatly different circumstances has, for a longer period than any other of Britain's sovereigns, fulfilled all the requirements of a very difficult position in a remarkable way, and at the moment is the object of respect, veneration and devotion which, gauged either in width, depth, and disinterestedness, or by nationalities, numbers, or power, the entire history of the world may look in vain for a parallel.

* An English chronicler of the time describes Boadicea as being of person tall, and of a cheerful, comely, and modest countenance. A Roman writer says "she was of the largest size, most terrible of aspect, most savage of countenance, and harsh of voice, having a profusion of yellow hair which fell far below her waist, and wearing a large golden collar. She had on a parti-coloured vest drawn close about her, and over this she wore a thick mantle connected by a clasp. Such was her usual dress, but at this time she also bore a spear, that she might appear more formidable."

PRODUCTION OF ILLUMINATED MANUSCRIPTS.

Most Englishmen have visited some of our picturesque and venerable cathedrals, or what remains of the abbeys or priories scattered over the land; and few have done so without being in some way moved, for they have a dignity and beauty, even when in ruins, which are impressive, and generally awaken thoughts about their origin and history, about some founder, ruler or inmate whose personality has left an impression. One indication of what was intended or done there, is the cloisters or scriptorium—either what remains of them or the place they occupied, is often examined with interest. What may be gathered of their purposes and uses seems the ground on which rests an opinion entertained, and sometimes expressed about illuminated manuscripts—that "they were made by the monks, who had plenty of time and nothing else to do." This is not strictly true, nor the whole truth. There were illuminated manuscripts before there were any monks; there were many produced in monasteries by those who were not monks, and who had not taken monastic vows. Many also were the work of those unattached to any monastery, working on their own account, or for a secular patron, who might be prince, noble, or commoner. And there were many made by women, both inside and outside of convents, actuated by the highest motives or by those of the typewriter of to-day.

It should be remembered that religious services in monasteries were seven times a day. Where these were strictly adhered to, little time was left, for those who took part in them, to write or illuminate manuscripts. We know that in the middle ages it was only in monasteries that a peaceful life and occupation could be led or followed, and as in the erection of many monasteries one object was the study and transcription of the sacred writings, so in the building of most of them provision was always made for a scriptorium, where they could be written or copied, and a library where they could be stored and studied. Not any monasteries but needed libraries, and few were without them, though sometimes the libraries contained few books and the scriptoriums were without workers; for not all of the religious orders attached equal importance to literature, or the ornamentation or illustration of books.

Charlemagne, in the encouragement given to Alchuine in aiding art and literature, we are told, had not only to overcome the objections of furious warriors, devoid of letters and almost of Christianity, who looked on such as unmanly, but of austere and ignorant monks who considered decoration in books as puerile. Long before him Benedict attached value to both, and when, in A.D. 539, he founded his Order he gave them special importance, making one of its objects the culture of science, and the transcription of books. So to the Benedictines more than any other order are science, literature and art indebted, and in their institutions there is fitter provision for their cultivation than in any other. The Carthusians, on the other hand, though an off-shoot or reformed branch founded by Bruno about 1100, and from the the 12th century in Britain next to the Benedictines in importance, as they were the builders of some of our finest structures, considered the illuminations of manuscripts to be at the best but elegant idleness, and discouraged such luxury, not allowing them to be produced, or even used in their houses; while in their stained windows colour was very sparingly used, generally only shades of grey crystallized in the style called *Camaïeu gris*. But with the Benedictines and others not only was it the practice to produce them, but their rules were elastic enough to admit any who could give artistic or other service, in exchange for the comfort and security which was then obtainable alone from them, because the power possessed by the Romish church and exercised over Europe during several centuries, and the prepossession in favour of monastic institutions had thrown in their lap immense wealth: so artistic knowledge and skill being unusual, and as the exercise of them was a benefit and honour to the Order and to religion, and a service to the entire church, the possessors of these powers were gladly received. As a French author says,—" In the abbeys and convents there were those who had taken no other vows than simply conforming to the rules, who purchased remission of their sins, not by long and painful penances, but, by enriching some of the books of the establishments with magnificent pictures, receiving in payment for services all the necessaries of life. They could in this way spend the greater part of a life in the decoration of a single book."

In the provision for the production of manuscripts in the more important monasteries there were the cloisters divided into *carrels*—square spaces—provided with light and comfort, where the illuminators could work alone, and the scriptorium, where copies could be made, or a number could write at one time from dictation. Depending upon the master or superior, so the scriptorium was either little used, or was often the scene of suitable decorous labour, made impressive by ceremonies as well as by permanent reminders and advice on the walls. There is a service-book, called a Benedictional, from containing a series of blessings to be invoked on various occasions, and one of them is intended to be used daily in the scriptorium—" Be pleased to bless, O Lord, this scriptorium of Thy servants and all those abiding therein, so that whatsoever shall be read or written by them from the Holy Scriptures, they may take it into their understanding and bring their work to a happy ending;" and at Martin du Tours there still remains some metrical advice composed by Alchuine for the school he established there, and where he reigned as abbot for eight years, and where he died and is buried:—

> "Let those that write these holy truths beware
> Their own vain words, that they insert not there,
> Nor falsely speak the text when thou shalt be
> Reader before the good fraternity.
> 'Tis better in transmitting books to toil
> Than seek to cultive and to delve the soil;
> Since he who is to meaner works confined
> May feed the body yet but starve the mind."

West gives the following picture of Alchuine as he presided over such a school, and the example which he wished followed wherever he had influence:—" In the hours set out for the copying of books the young monks file into the scriptorium, and one of them is given the precious parchment volume containing a work by Bede or Augustine, or else some portion of the Latin scriptures, or even a heathen author. He reads slowly and clearly at a measured rate while all the others, seated at their desks, take down his words, and thus perhaps a score of copies are made at once. Alchuine's observant eye watches each in turn, and his correcting hand points out the mistakes in orthography and punctuation. He makes himself the writing master of his monks, stooping to the drudgery of faithfully and gently correcting their many puerile mistakes, and all for the love of studies of Christ."

The work, both in the scriptorium and the *carrels* would, to any possessing a love of learning, or artistic taste and power, be a pleasant occupation, while to those engaged in the many long religious duties it would be a pleasant variety; while as, owing to those frequent religious services, those occupied with them could not give more than two hours at a time to writing or illuminating, such would be favourable and conduce to good work.* So when the scribe was not pressed for time; had pleasure in his work, for its own sake; felt it was an honour and benefit to his order and a duty and service to God, there is explanation enough why in many manuscripts there is an absence of any feebleness, and that every line and

* On showing the late Joseph Mayer a box decorated with pictures in enamel, with precious stones inserted, he remarked it could only have been slowly completed, to do it so well. "The worker could only have done a little at a time."

touch seems equally firm and delicate throughout. Though such would indicate it had been a labour of love, yet occasionally there are signs he was glad to get to the end of his task, for De Lisle quotes a scribe as writing, "Oh, what a heavy burden is writing! it curves the back, makes the eyes dim, breaks the stomach and ribs;" and another: "Friendly reader, keep your fingers off, lest you suddenly rub out the letters; for the man who knows not how to write can have no idea what a labour it is, since, just as the harbour is sweet to mariners, so is the last line to the writers. The reed is held with three fingers, the whole body works;" while a monk of St. Gallen says of one he wrote, that there was not a single leaf of parchment that he had not obtained by begging or by paying a high price, and not a letter nor a single point that was not traced by his own hand.

As a rule, the books produced in monasteries, whether by monks or those not under monastic vows, were subject to revision, the text collated, that it should be accurate, and that there should be propriety in the decoration; yet the illuminator who had any sense of humour or imagination—Waagen says, in England there was plenty of both—could even in monasteries, in the borders, exercise it and did, to his own enjoyment and that of his *confrères*, without much fear of censure, as the church then was tolerant of most things, excepting a direct attack on its interests. In other countries it was different. A Book of Hours esteemed harmless in France, where it was written, had to be, on entering Spain, examined, and a friar commissioned by the Inquisition notes that it had been corrected (some words inked and made illegible) and might be read.

Seeing the immense number of monasteries and monks, and the provision made for the production of books, one may wonder why they were so scarce—as there are many indications they were—during a great part of the Middle Ages, though met with statements of their abundance, such as that Winithar, a monk of St. Gall, about 780, during his life executed over seven hundred books, which would be more than one every month for fifty years. Errington thinks the number, both of monks and books, must be exaggerated— possibly there were errors in reckoning, not always intentional. Arithmetic is a weak point with many people now, and those who cannot read or write often reckon by twenties; so it could not be a strong point in the Middle Ages when so many were ignorant. Among many in monasteries there would be no practice or need in counting anything but their beads, as their individual possessions, on which arithmetic greatly rests, were limited to one or two articles. This may be one reason for errors in enumeration, as I have often thought, was why manuscripts were not regularly paged; and their order is only known by the catch-word at the bottom of every six, eight, sixteen, twenty-four, or more leaves, into which the skin of parchment was folded, being placed at the bottom of the series of "gatherings," as they were called. Almost the only manuscript that I have noticed as being paged at the time when it was written is a Missal I possess, written about 1400. Here the scribe has understood only counting by twenties, or thought the reader only would. He has certainly used L for 50, and C for 100, but nearly all the rest is so many twenties, the last leaf being marked $\frac{XX}{XIXXI}$, meaning nineteen twenties and eleven, or 391. This may not altogether be ignorance, but, though cumbersome, consecrated as part of the Roman notation of *Calendæ, Idus, Nonæ*, retained in the calendars.

So, up to the 12th century, the bulk of illuminated manuscripts that were produced were in monasteries, and, as was to be expected, were mainly Bibles, Psalters, Gospels, and books of theology; Books of Hours or Missals being non-existent up to that time. At any rate, according to Denis, such books were the only ones in France in which any picture of merit up to that time can be found, the reason being, not owing to the dignity of the subject or the motive inspiring the artist, but simply that monastic corporations possessed almost a monopoly of the wealth and power of the time. "They, only, could cause to be executed and pay for the masterpieces which are now the pride of our public institutions, for most noblemen were either absent on distant expeditions, or engaged in quarrels or feuds at home, which gave them little time and less money to spend on encouraging letters or art." But after the 12th century, from various causes, a taste for letters and a love of art sprang up, and a consequent demand for chronicles of History, Romances, Tales of chivalry and adventure, descriptions and representations of battles, tournaments, or any notable or national event. These the monasteries could not or would not supply but there were lay artists ready to do so. There was also the desire or ambition for a collection of books as a private library, and the Kings of France and others took into their service, or ranged among their retainers, scribes and artists who, to writing and illumination, could discharge other functions, or hold offices in their large establishments. By such artists many fine manuscripts were produced in France and Flanders, which is known, not by their names being affixed to them, but by accounts in books of their patrons, of payments or salaries paid to them. There were also artists of various kinds and grades, living by their profession, working for any who would employ them, alone or under a master, or as member of a society or guild, who met any demand by a supply according to the standard of what was required in quality and quantity. Often a manuscript was produced by division of labour, several taking part according to technical knowledge—one doing the simple writing, another the gilding, another the illuminated letter, another the complete picture or miniature—several different hands are often evident in the pictures that ornament one Missal or Book of Hours.

These guilds were not dissimilar to our own artistic societies, admittance being only obtained on proof of ability, and the membership gave certain privileges, even a monopoly, in certain localities. But with the privileges there were also certain duties—the guild granting the first and enforcing on the members the second.* And no doubt then, as now, there

* In the society of artists at Siena, in Italy, a fine was imposed on members who used debased gold, or blue colour made in Germany, which was inferior to the ultramarine, lapus lazuli, from Persia, or indigo from India.

were seasons when the members rejoiced together. In a copy of Froissart produced about 1400, and sold in the immense library of Rohan, Prince de Soulise, about 100 years ago, the writer of the manuscript had written these words at the end—

> Raoul Tanquy qui point n'est ivre,
> A Jamtem accomplit ce livre,
> La mardi quatrieme jour di Juillet,
> Puis alla boire chez Tabouret,
> Avec Pylon et autres Caterveaux,
> Qui aiment Ongnons, Trippes et aulx.*

As to the illumination of manuscripts, it should be noted, what is too much forgotten, that both in their writing and decoration women took an honourable part, not merely as lovers and enlightened patrons of all that was beautiful in art, such as Theodora, the wife of the Emperor Justinian, Charlemagne's favourite wife, his sister, daughter, and many more, but as artists, for art's sake or for a living. It is curious that

---

* This may be accepted as a translation :—
> I, Raoul Tanquy who never was drunk,
> Or hardly more than judge or monk,
> On fourth July finished this book,
> Then to drink at the Tabouret myself betook,
> With Pylon and boon companions more,
> Who tripe and onions, with garlick, adore.

As the 4th July ended what was probably a twelve months' labour, this pre-Raphaelite repast and its modest menu was as reasonable a celebration, though very different from a modern Academy dinner. Raoul was evidently a "clubbable man," and the character he gives himself for sobriety may not have been altogether for the sake of the rhyme, but be equally true as what Burns and Theodore Hook wrote of their heroes; but that honest Raoul wrote it 400 years before either of these Britons expressed the same sentiment is of interest, as shewing that "there is a deal of human nature in man."

the first name that has come down to us as occupied in the illumination of books is that of a female, a Greek, named, Lala de Cyzique, nearly a century before our era, who, having obtained a reputation as a painter of portraits, both on parchment and ivory, was induced by the learned librarian of Cæsar Augustus to decorate one of his books, in which she had the assistance of some young girls. Centuries afterwards several princesses are mentioned—the Princess Julienne, Gisela the wife of Stephen, King of Hungary, and Rathrade, daughter of the King of Lombardy. In the 6th century, a female saint, Radigunde, had a reputation that long remained. St. Columbkill, about the same time, tried to establish a convent specially for the purpose of women being instructed to practice the art. Denis says, "In the 9th to the 12th centuries it was a task imposed on the abbesses to copy and portray sacred symbols, and to paint the margins of books; and to ornament the sacred writings was to inform the mind and raise the soul to God. Painting in calligraphy was a consolation to many a great lady under suffering, and a complement to religious exercises. Such workers did much to preserve art from oblivion, when men gave their time and thoughts and found distraction in the shouts of battle or the disputes of the schools. Many names of female artists are given, more or less celebrated, though not any examples of their work remains, among them is Agnese, Abbess of Quedlinburgh, and member of a princely house, 1184-1205, and Herad, Abbess of Landsberg. On one manuscript, at Frankfort, the artist has left not only her name, but also her portrait, writing, " Guida paccatrix mulier scripsit and pinxit hunc librum." In 1324, there is the record of twenty-nine individuals being admitted as qualified writers by the college at Paris, and among them were two women. In the 15th century, the name of Elizabeth Mundapret, Cordelia Schoenean, and Dorothoee de Hof are on manuscripts. All know the eminent Flemish painter, Von Eyck, who was illuminator for the Emperor Charles V. His sister Margaret had an equal reputation which no doubt went to swell that of her brothers, for not any manuscripts remain that can be identified as exclusively her work. It is curious that one of the most eminent calligraphists of later times in our own country was Esther Inglis, whose family had to leave France, like many more Huguenots, and found refuge in Edinburgh. Ballard, who wrote about her, says, " Many others have been celebrated for their extraordinary talent this way, but this lady has excelled them all." Dr. Laing, of Edinburgh, who wrote an account of her, and gave some examples from manuscripts in the Bodleian, gives a list of many written by her and presented to the most important people of the time, Queen Elizabeth, the Earl of Essex, and Prince Henry, eldest son of James I, for whom she wrote two very small books, one in 1608, in Latin, the other 1612, in French. This latter is in the King of Sweden's library, the other I possess.

Of many Books of Hours offered for sale, I have seen only one specially indicating it was written by a female. It is Dutch, dated 1555, by Geertrudt van Doetinchem, who had given it to her sister, who again promised to any finder, in case of loss, "enen drinck pennie," for its safe return. It contains five miniatures occupying the full page, and the art exhibited is of average quality.

We have no information of what women did in England in early times in the illumination of manuscripts, but we may be certain they had a full share in building up the reputation of English illumination. This we can believe by the great value attached to their needlework pictures, which were mainly exhibited on ecclesiastical vestments. Many examples are now on the continent, preserved with care and shewn with pride, in Italy especially, by custodians, some ignorant, always unwilling to admit the English origin. Such work could not have been done unless the workers had power also with pen and pencil. Middleton says, "In the 13th century England surpassed the rest of the world in the art of embroidering delicate pictures in silk, especially for ecclesiastical vestments, and on many occasions the pope of this period, on sending the Pall to a newly elected archbishop, suggested that he would like to receive, in return, embroidered vestments of English work—*opus Anglicanum*."

THEIR VALUE IN THE MIDDLE AGES.

As to what was the cost of the illuminated manuscripts that now interest and charm us, or what was their value relative to other things in the time of their production, there is much difficulty in determining. The old chroniclers tell us of a good many things, but not any of them seem to think such information was worth giving to people of their own time, or that those coming after would ever care to know, so it is only from incidental references that we can form an idea of the value of books, either with or without illumination. Time, which is an important factor in the value of everything now, had a place of its own in monasteries. Then, of what entered into the production of illumimated manuscripts it was least considered, materials counted for more, and, perhaps, technical skill most of all. Writing or mere copying could be learnt, and copies made without the language being understood, which was done as is evident by the many clerical errors.* But artistic skill only exists when there is a union of natural aptitude and acquired knowledge, directed by aim and effort, which then and ever since are rarely combined. All the materials necessary for the production of an illuminated manuscript were expensive. Ink was often made from burnt ivory, gums were brought from Arabia, colours from Persia and India. Gold was much used in them, being applied in leaf form, much thicker than now, while ultramarine,—lapis lazuli—from Persia, was even dearer than gold, and the indigo from Bengal was also costly. In addition, parchment was very scarce. Though monks bound their own books, utilizing the skins of most animals, frequently of pigs, occasionally those of seals and sharks, and employing the precious metals with inlayings of still more precious stones, cut or uncut, they, as far as I know, did not make their own

* Jerome blamed the half learned who wrote down not what they found, but what they seemed to understand, and exposed their own blunders while they affected to correct the mistakes of others.

parchment, especially the very fine kind on which the best manuscripts were written. Such was only possible by organized and skilful labour, which might be thrown out of gear by war, foreign or domestic. This would partly account for its great cost at all times, and extreme scarcity generally. Middleton says, "Nothing is now made which resembles either the finest vellum of fifteenth century Italian manuscripts, or the exquisitily thin uterine vellum of the Anglo-Norman bibles, and that good vellum is only now made in Rome, and the quantity required for such as Caxton's *Golden Legend*," which may be compared with Farrar's *Life of Christ*, would cost now about £40. Up the 6th and 7th centuries, parchment, and paper from the papyrus plant in Egypt, were both used for writing, according to the importance of the document intended to be placed upon them. But when Egypt came into the possession of the Arabs, the supply of paper to Europe from papyrus ceased, and only parchment was available. Consequently, it became so scarce, that it was obtained by erasing writing already existing. This practice became so common, and so objectionable, that it was only stopped by something like a penal law. A French author says that there are few manuscripts of the 8th and 10th centuries remaining that are not of the kind called "palimpsest," from having been previously used. But this very scarcity and dearness caused the invention of paper from cotton or linen rags, and parchment, from about the 12th century, at least in France, became much more abundant. The large demand brought into existence a number of makers by whom the production was much increased, and who, according to the custom of the time, formed themselves into guilds, and obtained privileges, a status, and a recognition by local and central governments. In early times we do not hear of books being dealt with as merchandise, they are generally named as a gift to kings, emperors or churches. In later times such a gift was of sufficient importance to be marked by a courtly ceremonial or devotional service. In the latter case, whether Paul or Plato, it was placed on the altar as an acceptable offering. In some cases it was deemed worthy of mention on the tomb of the donor. When there is a sale mentioned, it is often by way of barter or exchange, sheep, land, or their products, sometimes silver, being the medium. Alfred the Great exchanged a small estate with the Abbot of the important Benedictine monastery of Monkwearmouth for a book on cosmography. In 1174, a monastery at Winchester exchanged with one at Dorchester twelve measures of barley and a silver embroidered pall for the Homilies of Bede and a Psalter of Augustine. Richard Bury, chancellor of Edward III, a true lover of books, gave 50 lbs. weight of silver for a number, and in 1430, Humphrey, Duke of Gloster, paid £1000, equal to twenty times as much now, for 120 volumes. The Countess of Anjou paid for a copy of the Homilies of Harmon two hundred sheep, five quarters of wheat, and the same of rye and millet. In 1453, a native of Bologna sold an estate to pay for a copy of Livy, and the seller bought another elsewhere with the money. Louis XI, of France, so well known by Scott's account of him in *Quentin Durward*, had to deposit a quantity of silver, give his personal security and that of a nobleman with him, before he could obtain the loan of a book from the Faculty of Medicine, at Paris. When manuscripts were produced by laymen, bills were rendered, and some of them remain. The account books of kings, popes and noblemen also sometimes shew what they paid to artists, in their service or occasionally employed by them, for the writing and decorations applied to books.

Myddleton gives the cost of several in the 14th century. An Evangeliarium cost £3 15s. 8d., equal to about £40 now. An Antiphonale £7 10s., equal to about £70, and a Lectionary at Bristol, in 1470, cost £3 4s. 1d , equal to about £20. Langlois says that at Rouen, a Missal about the same time cost about £40 or £50, though it was without miniatures, which would have added greatly to the cost. Among other prices mentioned, £250 was given for a copy of Livy, and £300 for one of the Golden Legend. A Bible for the Duke de Berri cost £1,600, and a Book of Hours of his was valued after his death, at 4,000 livres Tournois, equal to £2,000 now. One artist is named as receiving 54,000 francs for a Missal which occupied him eight years, and several others, retained by the popes, as having received what was about £25 to £30 per month.

The scribe sometimes gives his name, and states when he finished his book, but not so often when he began. One, however, mentions that it took him two years to write a Bible; another four years; and another was only ended after fifty years' labour. Another took four years to write a Missal;

another seven years to write a Breviary. The celebrated Julio Clovio was nine years over one. I have a small octavo copy of the epistles of Paul, written on paper, in 1584, by a monk in the Benedictine monastery of Mount Olivet, as a present to Cardinal Carafae. The writer, in his preface, says it occupied him six months. It is beautifully written, and has some arabesque borders, but is without miniatures. When months or years are mentioned as having been taken to produce any work, it cannot mean continuous labour of even eight hours a day, though necessity doubtless often compelled the lay scribe to labour so long, but the mere mention of the time would partly account for the scarcity of books and their high value.

Yet, seeing the great number of monasteries, the great number of inmates, the presence of a scriptorium, for the support of which estates were sometimes granted, we may wonder why they were so scarce. O'Dell Travers, writing in the *Gentleman's Magazine*, thinks that in the 13th century they were abundant, that there were book stalls and book sales, even lending libraries, in the chief towns of Europe at that time. He points as proof, to the library of Glastonbury which, he says, stood as high, if not higher, then than any monastery in England, as containing at that time 400 volumes, and that as many as fifty were copied there during the life of one abbot, which was, he adds, "a noble monument to the faithfulness of their devotion to the work of the scriptorium." But neither the number in the library of this, the most important establishment in Britain, nor the number copied — the time not stated — seems large or worthy of remark. It may be contrasted with statements that some of them had hardly any, some only one Missal. The scarcity and high prices would favour the opinion of Errington, who asks, "How did it happen, if the labour of the monks was so assiduous, considering the number of their establishments in all countries, that the copies of works were so scarce?" After reciting several reasons, "still the stubborn fact of scarcity inclines one to suspect that the pens of the monks were less constantly employed than many would induce us to believe. The scarcity then of books, of which innumerable proofs might be adduced, may be considered the cause of ignorance as well as the effect. We have, however, reason to be thankful that some were preserved, and I am not willing to withhold from the monkish labourers their due proportion of praise, however slender might be their pretensions."

There is some support given to this opinion by the fact that, when the writing and illumination of manuscripts was taken up by laymen, the number of Books of Hours and others, issued by guilds in France and Flanders, was very large, and, compared with the number from monasteries, seem in the same proportion as what is produced in a factory by modern machinery, and what was by hand labour in the old times.

CAUSES OF DESTRUCTION—INJURY.

"Change and decay in all around we see" is certainly true of every human work. An architect told me that a building is no sooner completed than it begins to decay. Moths attack the finest tissues; delicate carvings in wood the worm; artistic creations in gold and silver are often a prey to the vulgar thief, who reduces them to so much metal; atmospheric changes, wear and tear, accidents and neglect do much, but wilful destruction perhaps more. This has levelled many a proud palace and strong castle, as it has been fatal to many a beautiful manuscript, the creation of much patient labour and skill.

It has been already noted that art and religion, of some kind, are often companions, giving each other aid and exercising a mutual influence. With the Jews, their religion had the first place; art was secondary with the Mohammedans, indeed, was hardly recognised. But with the Greeks, art was supreme. Christians have acted like both. One section of them taking the Jewish view, another the Greek, and both giving reasons and warmly defending their opinions and practice. Both may be right in principle, but both have been wrong or intolerant in its extreme application, almost in proportion to their sincerity. The feeling is perfectly natural that to what is sacred all honour should be rendered, equally so is it that the Deity, being a spirit, can only be worshipped in spirit and truth, and his honour not given to another.

The Greek practice was adopted by that section of the Christian church of which Rome is the fountain head; the Jewish by the iconoclasts, and applied in the 8th century, as it was at the Reformation in the 16th century. It is also the one accepted now by all to whom the scriptures are a law and the final court of appeal. So it was on the two occasions named, and at those times that a great, the greatest, destruction of illuminated manuscripts took place. In A.D. 724, the Emperor Leo began his memorable crusade against them by destroying the image of Christ, which Constantine had set up over the principal entrance of Constantinople; other statues and figures of saints followed, and ultimately all copies of the sacred writings containing decorations or pictures. The library there, which is supposed to have contained then 50,000 volumes of them, was set on fire, and that number burnt, among them were many unequalled for all that makes a book valuable, the writing, illumination and binding. This destruction by the head of the state drew with it many in private hands, either from a desire to obey the law, from fear of the consequence of disobedience, or from policy and to curry favour. The destruction was evidently very complete, because, of all the beautiful books produced at Rome by Greek, Sicilian or Italian artists, during several centuries, none remains now even of those executed for the immediate predecessors of Leo. The orders were carried out, not only in the eastern empire, but in the west, as far as his power or influence extended, for in 728, he ordered the Exarque of Ravenna to act in the same way, and to break down the images in all the churches in Italy. The Pope at that time, Gregory II, felt himself compelled to threaten excommunication to avert what he thought would be injurious to art and religion. The opinions and acts of Leo in the matter were shared and acted on by his successors, with few intervals, for about one hundred and fifty years, so the destruction of good examples was so great, the discouragement during that long time was so complete, that when a compromise was arrived at, and toleration, within certain limits, was the rule, artists had comparatively to go again to school, and only by degrees did they recover their power and reputation.

In the west, wherever the church of Rome had influence, there was a different action, images, pictures and decorations of all kinds were encouraged and used in the church and its service, and continued until the Reformation, when, wherever the sacred writings were permitted, and the Bible circulated in the vulgar tongue, and its teaching followed, the sentiments of the iconoclasts took form and action, and the destruction of illuminated manuscripts in England was great and deplorable. Old chronicles tell how " soldiers of Henry VIII, and of Cromwell, tore a whole library of service books into fragments, and rolled knee deep in them," or how "glovers supplied themselves with vellum to wrap up their wares, or bakers to feed their ovens."

While the destruction of images and also of illuminated manuscripts in Britain was greatly owing to the belief that they were unscriptural it must have been partly owing to their being in Latin and not understood, for it is difficult to believe, from the religious character of the English, that Gospels, Psalters, etc., would not, being sacred writings, have found that sufficient for protection, had they been in English. So that as pictures in the first instance were thought necessary to make the text understood and attractive, they were inadequate when present to save it from destruction when in an unknown tongue.

This view has some support from the fact noted that in some cases parish registers were destroyed by the Puritans because, being in Latin and not readable, it was thought they must be full of "Popery and treason." There is a tradition regarding registers in Ireland that "were burnt because they were in Latin, and the simpletons who gained possession of them came to the conclusion they were 'rebel muster rolls.'"—*Athenæum*.

The progress of the Turks in Europe was also the cause of the destruction of many; among others, the magnificent library of Matthias Corvinus, of Hungary, perished when his capital was taken by them.

Beyond what manuscripts of Christian writings were destroyed by Puritans, many most valuable belonging to the Arabs in Spain, as also many of much interest in the history of human progress in Mexico, were destroyed by the catholic bishops, who, using art greatly themselves, did not then, nor does their church now, tolerate anything in text or ornament that seems to question their decrees or teaching. Even so recently as one hundred years ago, manuscripts of all kinds, of every age, in immense quantities, perished in the ferment of the French Revolution. In this case, it was not zeal for the purity of religion that was the moving power, but more the absence of any belief in it, or from actual hatred of its restriction, or more frequently the pure greed of gain: the clasp or covering of a manuscript, if of any intrinsic value, being sufficient cause for its destruction.

Langlois says, "I have seen at the time of the Directory, within the walls of Paris, a great number of vellum books, curious for their antiquity, and the decorations on them, torn up, and used by the government in making cartridges, and what I saw done there, was being done all over France, for guns of heavy calibre. And for a long time, ignorant and illiterate men were seen hunting for, and procuring somehow, enormous packages of vellum manuscripts, to be used, without examination, in various ways connected with machinery." "Even as late as 1825," he says, "the authorities of Rouen gathered out of various garrets in the Hotel de Ville, where they had been exposed to all kinds of injuries, about 1,200 thick volumes of manuscripts, and had them placed in the city library. The Abbé Lespine, Directeur d'Ecole des Chartes, says that, 'many ancient manuscripts of Chapters and Abbeys have been cruelly thrown into cellars or garrets, where they slowly perished, and became food for worms or rats.' He has seen this during several journeys he made in the south of France."

Besides what has been named as causing the total destruction of illuminated manuscripts, there are other reasons for their being seldom perfect. It might be expected that in the long interval since they were produced much of their original brightness would be gone. That is so, and many are a mere wreck of their former selves, partly from actual use in devotional services, sometimes at the hands of children, when given them to play with, or to keep them quiet. Two of mine have been so maltreated, one, apparently, by a wet finger, another by a pin applied to the faces of the figures. One of the most valuable and interesting of those in the British Museum is the Bedford Missal. For some years it was in the possession of Sir John Tobin, of Liverpool. His grandson told me he often had it when a child, he didn't say to play with, but to look at; and an old gentleman told me he often dined with Sir John, and after dinner the Missal was always brought out for the inspection of the guests. Fortunately, it escaped injury, and is wonderfully perfect, which, from the care now taken, seems assured for all time.

Beyond the injury that many manuscripts have sustained through carelessness and neglect, many are terribly mutilated through some miniature or ornament being cut out by some vulgar thief, and sold ultimately to be framed or added to something else at the caprice of the buyer. As a matter of course, the better the example was, the more danger it ran of being torn from its position. So many Books of Hours have been treated in this way, that few are absolutely perfect, and only those acquainted with them, and Latin scholars, can tell in the absence of any original pagination that there is any abstraction. I have seen several collections of miniatures, etc., that once ornamented Books of Hours, put up in a scrap book. To see them away from their natural surroundings and associations struck a note of sadness like the wail of the Jews at the waters of Babylon, or the sight of Saxon children slaves in the streets of Rome. In one sale there were offered in various lots more than 700 miniatures, which probably deprived nearly 100 Books of Hours of the best ornaments in them, and took away what to most people constituted their value.

A bookseller told me he had sold many examples of the lower priced Books of Hours to artists, who, at the time of the pre-Raphael movement, obtained from them models for figures in their pictures.

Owing to these various causes Books of Hours and other manuscripts, in good preservation and complete, are very rare, either of those offered for sale or what we see in private possession.

ECCLESIASTICAL USE OF LATIN—ITS INFLUENCE.

We all know that Latin has been the language used by the Church of Rome for its many purposes during the long period of 1500 years. But as it was a dead language during all that time, there must have been reasons for its retention.

Its influence in many respects has been so considerable, that something on the point may be permitted to be said, even in a sketch like this.

To do this, we must recall that when Christianity was introduced, Rome was the chief city in the world. The Romans were masters of the greater portion of what was civilized, and Latin was their language. Professor Wey describes it as one of those that soon arrive at perfection, and soon die. (Tenhove says it began to decline within two hundred years after attaining perfection.) "Elegant, concise, and sonorous, it was constructed with almost mathematical accuracy and was very difficult. On that account it was only fitted for small communities, and quite unfitted for actual use by the many different peoples of which the Roman empire was composed.* The difficulties of the language," he says, "were so great, that at the height of the Roman grandeur, the empire of pure Latin was bounded by the gates of the Capital. It was too delicate for what was needed, and was really killed by the rapid growth of the empire, and like Sanscrit, it soon passed into the condition of a monument, to be a language consecrated to dogmas and mysteries, preserved by priests as the one is at the foot of the Himalayas, where it was born, the other in the city of the Cæsars and of St. Peter." A Christian church was early formed in Rome, and for its use a service or liturgy made up of prayers, hymns, and portions of the sacred writings was in that language. The entire Bible was also translated into it from Greek. In course of time the Roman empire was broken up, and Latin ceased to be spoken or intelligible excepting to students. Nevertheless, the church at Rome continued to retain its liturgy, and the Bible in that tongue. As ages rolled on, that

* In the life of Nicholas Breakspear, the only English Pope (1154), Adrian IV, it is stated that some cardinals sent by him to Frederic Barbarossa, Emperor of Germany, to settle a dispute, used the word "beneficia," which spiritually meant "blessing," but also "temporal property," and the Pope was understood to claim for himself as being the power from which the Emperor and Princes derived their possessions, and by whom they could be conveyed to others, as he had done Ireland to the King of England. Though the Emperor had previously humbled himself to hold the Popes stirrup, he drew the line here, and invaded Italy. The Pope on his side prepared to defend himself by using his spiritual power of excommunication, but died before there was collision.

church, through various causes, especially through claims based on the sacred writings or their interpretations, attained a power that in religion was supreme, and in politics hardly less. That power always employed it for all purposes, and was able to cause the liturgy and bible to be kept in Latin, and also to prevent them being translated into the mother tongue of any nation. That the Papacy should retain and use Latin when it had ceased to be intelligible, even in Rome, and was a dead language everywhere else, is a singular incident in history.

The reasons usually put forward or given for the course adopted are: If Latin had not been retained as a sacred language, and as it were the depository of that truth and science, it would have been lost in the barbarous dialects of the vulgar. That the use of Latin had the effect of preserving all ancient Latin literature that otherwise would have been lost, and provided a mode of communication between the learned of all countries, as it was the medium in which for centuries their thoughts were mainly given to the world. That the bible translated by Jerome into Latin was like a copy of a lost original, attested by one of the most eminent fathers, and by the general consent of the church. That many of the prayers and hymns of the early Latin Christians are in that language, the musical chants were adapted to those sounds, and depended for their effect on the marked accents and powerful rhythms which the Latin language affords, so that veneration, and a natural dislike of innovation, conspired to retain them, even after the language had so changed that the words to the multitude had lost their meaning. That to allow the Bible to be translated into the vulgar tongue would permit errors to creep in, false interpretations to be given, and heresies to arise.

After reviewing these, Hallam adds, "When Latin ceased to be intelligible, every principle of religious worship called for the scriptures and liturgy being translated out of it—there was no sufficient reason why they should not, and that the policy of keeping them in it was the cause of the ignorance of the people and the gross corruption of the middle ages."[*] And Wey says, "So Latin was the safeguard of the unity of the church. Virgil, Horace and Cicero had worked for Saint Jerome." If the sacred writings had not been retained in Latin, and through that kept practically as sealed books, it is not easy to see how the papacy would have acquired and exercised the power it has done for so many centuries. It seems probable, that had the Bible been translated into the various languages which the people of Europe were using, every nation would have been supplied with a book superior, even in a literary point of view, to any classic ever written.[†]

[*] In *History of Rome in the Middle Ages*, Gregorovius gives a terrible picture, saying, "From the highest to the lowest, whether laity or clergy, the only form of religion was that of a gross superstition." The Gallic Bishops, in the 10th century, declared, "there is no one at present in Rome who has studied the sciences. The ignorance of other priests is in some degree pardonable, when compared with that of the Bishop of Rome. In him, ignorance is not to be endured, since he has to judge the universal Catholic Church."

[†] An unimpassioned critic in the *Athenæum*, quite recently, says, "Every one of us is agreed that, quite apart from its theological or antiquarian interest, the Bible contains some of the masterpieces of the world's literature. For rapid, for clear narrative, for pathos, for irony, for homely wisdom, it can compare on

A book of which the influence would have been entirely favourable, not only to morals, but also to education, the formation of a national literature and progress generally; while, though the Bible was not given to teach secular knowledge, which man can acquire as needed from experience, yet it does give what would have been antidote to many classical errors* which the exclusive study of Greek and Latin perpetuated for centuries, and also would have combated many purely literary grounds with anything Hellas or Rome can shew; and the curious thing is that these qualities can be transferred almost entirely without loss from the original to translation. Quite from a secular standpoint the authorized version is the greatest prose masterpiece of English literature, while both modern German language and literature date from Luther's Bible." Wey says, " Luther changed the religion of Germany in giving that country, as the first model of the regenerated language, a translation of the Bible."

* The making of Latin a sacred language, and consequently directing the thoughts and study of the finest minds upon Latin and Greek authors, had the effect of investing their works with something of an inspired character and of creating a feeling that to doubt the opinions of Aristotle, Pliny, or Ptolemy, was almost the sin of heresy. There is little doubt but that in monastic retreats, or other places of study, there were many things known or discovered beyond what Roger Bacon † or Galileo did, that fell into disuse, were discouraged, or actually stifled, more owing to their being contrary to profane authority than from being opposed to the sacred writings, and that decisions embodied and accepted as infallible, were perhaps sometimes arrived at, owing to the unconscious bias which members of the conclave had received from acute minds with whose opinions, in the elegant languages of Greece or Rome, they were familiar. We know that the ideas of classical authors about astrology and the influence of the stars, the nature, origin and power of precious stones, and the form and shape of the earth, as well as regards medicine and natural history, were accepted and universal among the learned of the middle ages down to a very recent period.

Regarding astrology and the influence of the planets—the belief in which was long so universal, and is not yet extinct—it may be traced through Zadkiel,

† A French author says, "Roger Bacon, the greatest genius England ever possessed, surrounded by spies and monks, was accused, tormented, condemned and paid by ten years imprisonment for the crime of not being understood and being before his time."

beliefs and practices of savage people, which, while in an unknown tongue, it could not touch. Various claims of the papacy also, such as divine power, infallibility, would probably never have been made, certainly would have been examined, and being so, would not have been accepted, to the same extent, and the history of the world would have been different.

Had the Bible been in the vulgar tongue, one result would

Old Moore, King and others up to Lilly, who, a writer says, "stole his farrago of rubbish, &c., from monkish chronicles, as they got them from the Greek and Roman writers." In the *Gentleman's Magazine* for 1843, there are extracts from the manual of a monk or parish priest of the 15th century, which comprised grammar, prayers, forms for wills leaving property for pious purposes and the good of souls, and also a treatise on judicial astronomy, "without which no astronomer, philosopher, surgeon or any other could worke his craft,"—which said book was composed "in the londe of Greece, by the wisest philosopher that ever existed." Among other things, the monk goes through the signs of the Zodiac, giving extraordinary reasons for their names, and defining their influence, which was all powerful on the character, disposition and fate of those born under them. After various quotations from this manuscript, the commentator adds, "One ceases to wonder at the darkness which overspread the Christian church in our land before the reformation of her services and translation of the Bible, when one finds such specimens of theological deduction as in the passages cited. Nor is divinity, if I am rightly informed, of a much higher order at the present day in Italy, and other parts of the continent."

This opinion derives some support from a reported revision lately made of the books in the Index Expurgatorious, from which, by orders of the Pope, some were omitted, but others were added, especially various works on astrology. In the printed Books of Hours, about A.D. 1500, there is the representation of the figure of a skeleton, with astrological information; and in a British almanack for 1739, among information about fairs, &c., is one "Now advise with the honest and able astrological physician."

Regarding precious stones, I may mention that many years ago I was much interested in what was said by ancient authors regarding their origin and powers. They were considered mysterious things, as descended from the stars, sometimes as being living things, male and female, and invariably as possessing supernatural powers. These were the opinions of those who had written about them, whether

have been that printing would have been invented earlier, and its benefits obtained centuries before they were.* It may be urged these ideas are mainly speculative, but there is support for them in what has been seen in Europe for centuries, and in other countries for shorter periods, by the working of the

Greek, Roman or Arabian writers including early Christians, Saints and Popes, and remained dominant until a late period, being repeated in a book, published at Oxford, of all places, about 200 years ago. The only book that, while mentioning them, did not countenance these beliefs, was the Bible, where, though referred to often in one or other of the many books of which it is composed, precious stones are never mentioned in any other way, otherwise than as rare and beautiful things, always spoken of in terms such as a man of science, in any popular account, would use in the present day, and never as possessing any supernatural powers. The impression left with me was, that classical opinions had been accepted regarding them, either preferring them to the Bible, or from sheer ignorance of what it said about them. How the Bible had dealt with the influence of both the stars and precious stones, directly or by inference, in comparison with all other authors, up to a recent date, ought to add to the evidence in favour of a divine origin.

As regards geography, classic opinions also held the field until the last few hundred years, and no doubt acted, if not in discouraging adventure, at least in directing it and scientific enquiry into wrong channels. Even up to the last hundred years, what Ptolemy said about the coast line of Lancashire was considered gospel.

The river Mersey he placed about thirty miles north of where it is now, and where, his followers said, like the man in the stocks, it has no right to be. That it had taken such a course and is there, seemed to them an irregular proceeding on the part of the river, and quite unfair to the old Greek. But a gentleman living on the banks of the Mersey, as well acquainted with Greek as Ptolemy, and knowing the river a great deal better, took up his calculations, and shewed he was in some of them wrong; among others, that he had reckoned a degree as sixty miles when it is nearly seventy. By carefully considered data and calculations, he seems to prove that the river, though something changed, as should be expected in the time—mainly through wear and tear—runs much in the same course as it did eighteen hundred years ago.†

* It has always seemed to me that printing was on the verge of being discovered and utilized long before it was, nor is it easy to understand why it was

† The *Geography of Ptolemy Elucidated*, by Thomas Glazebrook Rylands, 1893.

two opposite systems. The one where the Bible is in a living language understood by the people, or the other where it is only allowed in one which is dead and unknown to them. Up to the 15th century, Rome prevented any people having the Bible in its mother tongue. At that time, several nations, among them England, rebelled against such prohibition, and had it translated into the language of the people and given to them. Several did not, but continued without it. Among them was Spain, at that time the most powerful nation in Europe, and far superior to England. At present, and for a century past, Spain is a very second rate power, infinitely inferior in every respect to England, which possesses and exercises an influence greater than any nation ever before. Competent observers ascribe much of that power to the possession of the Bible, and fix the beginning of that power to be the time when it appeared in the language

not, seeing that for hundreds of years the kernel of the art was possessed and actually used whenever an ordinary seal was applied. The probability is that printing of a kind was known but not encouraged or actually prohibited.

When the production of books got into the hands of lay scribes, the object then, as much as it is to day, was to produce them rapidly, and that in itself was leading and preparing the way for mechanical aid. Printing was first used in the production of playing cards, which, when introduced, spread rapidly, and their manufacture was an important source of wealth both to Germany and Venice. The devices on them being stamped like seals, led to engraving, and were followed by printing on paper, which differed from seals or engraving only in this, that the seal or stamp was one design, but in printing the parts or individual letters were separable and allowed of combinations. Wey says, "Those who received cards with eagerness under the passion for play, did not suspect that in this new game lay the germ, the first cause, of the two finest inventions of the human mind, engraving and printing. Playing cards no doubt circulated a long time throughout the world before the public voice announced the almost simultaneous engraving on wood and metal and printing."

of its people, and that it is mainly owing to the translation then made, that English literature is so copious and so valuable, and that the language of England seems destined to become universal and to supersede all others.* The experience of England with savage people everywhere is also, that giving them the Bible in their own tongue is the readiest and best means of raising them morally and intellectually. Within about a century the Bible has been translated by England into between five and six hundred different languages. In India alone during the last eighty years into about forty, the result in all cases being so encouraging that about a thousand men are constantly employed in the work of translation.

However, the point mainly to be considered in this paper is what influence the exclusive use of Latin had on art generally, especially the illumination of manuscripts, which, as far as I know, has not hitherto been noticed.

We have seen that, before writing was invented, pictures served the purpose in an imperfect way, and we know that whenever or wherever the language is unknown, pictures or representations are again necessary, and must be resorted to for explanation. So to use an unknown tongue must tend to

* Dr. Schiver has been considering the need of an universal language, and says, "There is one already. It is English. It is spread over the whole world and is easily learned. It has obtained a position so far in advance of others that neither natural nor artificial means can deprive it of it. It is spoken by the most powerful nation in Europe, in the greater part of N. America, S. Africa, Australia and in India. Since the beginning of the 19th century, the number of English-speaking people has grown from twenty-five millions to one hundred and twenty-five millions, and there is no prospect of any check."

create and make almost necessary a large use of art to convey an idea of what is desirable. And we can understand the increased use of pictures, statues, signs, symbols, processions, etc., pleasant and agreeable in themselves, and that, wherever possible, the ecclesiastical buildings of the Roman church would become imposing, the ritual striking, the music moving, while pictures and decorations on walls and windows would add to the effect, telling to the eye what the dead language could not. Pictures, therefore, were not only permanently inside the church, occasionally on the walls surrounding it, but they were also sometimes exhibited from the pulpit. Langlois says, " In the times when noblemen were hardly less ignorant than their serfs, a custom suited to those barbarous times prevailed of employing the talents of Greek or Italian calligraphers to paint what was called 'Exultet' (from the first word of the hymn 'Exultet jam turba'). These were paintings on leaves of vellum fastened together. The preacher, while he recited the Latin hymn, unrolled these pictures, so that the figures on them explained to the people the meaning of the words he had spoken." He says these were in use in the kingdom of Naples until the end of the 16th century, and that something similar was used in France and Flanders to represent by pictures the events of the Apocalypse.

In the middle ages few could read their mother tongue, let alone Latin. For the mass, there was little object in learning that, as there was little effort to induce them to learn. So what was known of the Bible by the body of the people was obtained from pictures in the churches, dramatic representations, miracle plays, or the sermons of preaching friars. The rich who could afford them had pictures in books—the Bible and Psalter in early times—so when Horae or prayer books became more general, as they were less bulky and expensive, there were pictures in them, partly for adoration, but mainly because the text was in a language not understood. Those who knew the language in which they were written did not need pictures, but to the laity who could not read it, such pictures were not only agreeable to the eye, and an incentive to devotion, but were almost necessary. Consequently, it is not in Missals, or any other books used by the priest, but in Books of Hours, the prayer book of the laity, that we find the greatest number of pictures and the most profuse illustrations and illuminations. So that, keeping the principles of Christianity and the service and ministration of it in a dead language, one not understood by the people, was not bringing religion to them, so far as conveying instructions by the best and easiest methods was concerned, but was practically returning to the practice of using pictures, as was done when writing was unknown.* The result, directly or indirectly, was that art, in the practice of the papacy, assumed much the

* The poet Wordsworth was not favourable to pictorial literature. On the appearance of the *Illustrated News* (1846) he said:

"A backward movement surely have we here,
From manhood back to childhood; for the eye
Back towards caverned life's first rude career.
Avaunt this vile abuse of pictured page!
Must eyes be all in all, the tongue and ear
Nothing? Heaven keep us from a lower stage!"

position it did with the Greeks and Romans. This was seen in Italy, which attained an excellence in art previously reached only by Greece in its best days, and was reached in Italy by art taking the first place, and religion a second.

A living illustration of this was Pope Leo X. The patron of Raphael, Michael Angelo, and some of the highest names in art, the chief builder of the most important Christian temple in the world, St. Peter's, at Rome, where art of every kind is profusely displayed; he employed most objectionable means, by selling indulgencies, to obtain money for the purposes and objects of the various forms of art in which he delighted.

Dean Church says, "To whole generations of the Italian people the worship of the beautiful, as the noblest and worthiest devotion, stood in the place of truth, morality, of Christian life, and this idolatry of beauty brought its own punishment, the degeneracy and deep degeneration of both art and character." For a long time, Italy, especially in regard to education, and even in regard to art, has not compared favourably with other nations.

It is then the case that much art has come down to us, in illuminated manuscripts among others, and that it is of a certain kind and form is owing to the impulse and direction given by the church of Rome, very much because it has chosen that Latin, during many centuries, should be the exclusive language.

By that church, in its services, pictures and decorations are more largely employed than by any other body of

Christians, as they will continue to be where the feelings and emotions are more considered than the intellect and reason, and as they must be so long as a dead language, and not the mother tongue of the audience is mainly used.*

BOOKS OF HOURS.—WHAT THEY ARE.

A "Book of Hours," "Horæ" or "Offices" † is practically a prayer book, yet it is much more than a collection of Collects, which the title "Prayer Book" strictly implies. It contains less matter than our Book of Common Prayer, is not, like it, invariably the same in all examples, and in other respects differs greatly. For instance, in both there is a Litany, and some phases and petitions are common to both, but in the Book of Hours, prayers to the persons of the Deity are few, while to the Virgin, Angels, and Saints they are many, who are addressed by name in the short request *ora pro nobis*, pray for us. The Litany, in the Book of Common Prayer, on the other hand, is a series of prayers, brief, yet applicable to all circumstances and conditions of life. They address and appeal direct to the persons of the Trinity, but to no other. The Prayer Book also contains Communion, Baptismal, Matrimonial, and other services, which are entirely

---

* "The object of 'Old Catholics' in separating from the Church of Rome is to return to the doctrines and discipline of the ancient and undivided church, of which vernacular services in public worship is one."

† Tite says "all 'Offices' may be regarded as 'Hours,' yet all 'Hours' are not 'Offices,' but at an early period in the history of typography the term 'Horæ' or 'Hours' became a general term for a certain class of decorated books of devotion. So in reference to Illuminations, 'Hours' and 'Offices are spoken of as one and the same book." The English name was "Primer."

absent from the Book of Hours, and only found in books appertaining to the priestly office called Missal, Pontifical, &c.

The Book of Psalms, or "Psalter," means a compilation of canticles or songs, which it truly is, the last word in it being the comprehensive invitation, "Let every thing that has breath praise the Lord," but it is also much more, for in many of the Psalms it is difficult to say whether prayer or praise most preponderates. Certainly, the Book of Psalms has ever been the great storehouse from which prayer, as well as praise, has been drawn, as in it, more than other books, do we realise the existence of one, Infinite and Almighty in every attribute of Power and Goodness, and find words in which finite beings can venture to address Him in prayer, praise, and adoration. John Bright would stake upon the Book of Psalms the great question, whether there is or is not a divine revelation, and most of those who come to it without prejudice, and give it careful examination, arrive at the same conclusion. It was the prayer book from the beginning of Christianity and well down the ages; but in time there were added to it the Magnificat, the Confitebor, and the Te Deum, while, as the Divinity of the Virgin, the worship of images, the intercession of saints, the power of indulgencies, were decreed and accepted, compositions in which they were embodied were added, and the Psalter in its entirety as a prayer book disappeared.* It is these various compositions,

---

* Individual Psalms are constantly used in Books of Hours. Of the seven called Penitential Psalms a special service is made, as, in some cases, are those called "Graduale" or of Degrees.

united with extracts from the sacred writings, brought together, that form the Book of Hours which ousted the Psalter* from the place it long held, and took its position as the prayer book of the laity.† The Book of Hours usually contains sixteen sections. The service for the dead was, perhaps, the first to be formed, but that of the Virgin was the most important, and often gives a title to the entire book and causes it to be called "Hours of the Virgin." The first step

* When it is said the Psalter was the Prayer Book, that means it was the chief portion of the Prayer Book. Then the daily service was divided into seven hours. In each there were accompanying prayers and hymns, generally one or other after each Psalm. So the entire Psalter, which in the English Prayer Book is gone through in a month, was, in all the dioceses of England, then gone through in a week. The Psalter was in the one form in Sarum, Hereford, and York, but the Latin hymns used with it differed, each diocese having some preferences. It is probable that the Psalter, as used at Sarum about A.D. 1,500, was much the same, or little altered, from the time of Augustine. The Litany in the Sarum Psalter is greatly superior to the baldness of that in ordinary Continental Books of Hours, and it was from it that many of the beautiful prayers in the Litany of the English Prayer Book were taken.

† No doubt at all times, more, perhaps, in England than on the Continent, there were prayers or collections of prayers made and used by private persons, apart either from the Psalter or Book of Hours. In the British Museum there is the fragment of a layman's Prayer Book of the 14th century. It contains a medieval version of the Lord's Prayer, the Te Deum, &c., in English. The Pembroke Book of Hours, written about 1,440, contains prayers composed by Katherine Parr, and added about 100 years afterwards. I have a manuscript, dated 1,555, written for a Princess of Savoy, which is entirely of prayers to saints, each being preceded by a representation of the one addressed. Another is a *Précis*, or epitome of the Prayer Book used by the Emperor Charles V. It begins with a Litany to the Virgin and the Holy Sacrament, contains a prayer daily used by the Emperor, and concludes with "*Sentenze e Versetti di salmi da seruirsi per aspirationi nelli principali attioni del giorno.*" The celebrated Jarry wrote many Prayer Books for private use; in one case he complained that he was ashamed of the silliness he was sometimes required to write.

in the formation of that service was in the 5th century, when the worship of the Virgin as the mother of God was decreed by the Council of Ephesus. In the 9th century her effigy first appears on the coins of a Greek Emperor, and in the 10th century *Ave Maria* began to be added to the Lord's prayer, and used with it, while in the next century it was formally introduced into the offices of the Church.

In the 11th and 12th centuries, a great impulse and decided direction was given to art and religion throughout Europe by the crusades and the many pilgrimages to the Holy Land. Legends and apochryphal gospels by these were brought thence and spread widely, to be read or seen and heard everywhere in pictures, ballads, miracle plays, and religious dramas, which were gradually incorporated into the teaching of the church.

In the 13th century, a deep, almost passionate, devotion to the Madonna is evident by the appearance, among other things, in localities widely separated, of pictures breathing the one spirit, as if emanating from one mind.

In the 14th century, the worship of the Virgin greatly increased, and the title of "our Lady" became general. It was not merely religious, but was colored by the chivalric character of the period. There was even rivalry among religious bodies as to which could do her most honour. The Cistercians, proud to be enrolled as her servants, adopted white as an appropriate livery. The Servi, or servite, *esclaves de Marie*, black, for the same reason. The Franciscans stand out as the champions of the Immaculate Conception; and the

Dominicans introduced the rosary; while churches, chapels and pictures in her honour greatly multiplied.* A special Litany was composed for her, in which, under about forty different titles, she was addressed, "Ora pro nobis," and the "Te Deum" was made to apply specially to her. As to when the Book of Hours first appeared in complete form there is not agreement. Though some prayers or services found in them were the production of individual Popes, yet the bulk of the book seems to have grown up and been shaped by fraternities or local synods, which explains why there is not exact uniformity, but the form varies in different localities, and is described as being "according to the use of Rome, Paris, Rouen, Sarum, etc." †

In the 13th century, Christianity had been accepted all over Europe. Population and wealth had also greatly increased, and the power of the church and its religious orders was paramount. A prayer book was needed by the laity and in the interests of the church, one containing what had been decided they ought to know, or were permitted to know, was very desirable. So about that time Books of Hours must have arisen, for though in the large collections of the British Museum there are illuminated manuscripts as early as the 6th century, there are not any Horæ earlier than the

---

* Mrs. Jameson.

† I have one which states it is according to the use of the Carthusians, and another that of the preaching friars. Searle and James both point out wherein "the use of Rome," Paris, &c., differ from each other. These points are sometimes the only indication where, or in what diocese, a Book of Hours was produced.

14th. Searle says they are hardly known in the 13th, and are very rare in the 14th. But when they appeared, being made up of short detached services taken from the psalter, breviary, etc., suitable for use in chamber or oratory, portable and convenient, and often accompanied by promises of indulgencies* for the performance of one or other of their services, they were acceptable and became popular. In the same proportion, the Psalter as a prayer book was laid aside, and, as Middleton says, "In the 15th century, the influence of the church tended to check the study of the Bible, that also was much disused, on the part of the laity. Very few of them were then written, but immense numbers of Horæ." Contributing to this was the fact that such were written and illuminated by laymen for laymen, who paid for and could direct the style, the ornaments, even the services they preferred, or the saints they esteemed; and so it happens that Books of Hours, the outcome of changes in society and circumstances, clerical and secular, are the most abundantly illuminated of theological books of the middle ages, and the most interesting, in regard to art, and the best known.

* From an addition in a later hand to an Italian Book of Hours, I learn that the Hours of the Holy Cross were established by Pope John XXII (1316-1334), and that he granted a year's indulgence to whoever said them. He it was who, being asked by the other cardinals to name a Pope to succeed Clement V, named himself, saying, *Ego sum Papa*. Blair says John wished to interfere in the affairs of Scotland, which as Robert Bruce would not allow, he was excommunicated in consequence; that John's ambitious schemes left Italy distressed and impoverished, but his own treasury full. The fifteen OO's were composed at the end of the 14th century by St. Bergetta, of Sweden, who used to say them at the door of St. John Lateran.

The word "Office" means much the same as our word "service," and "Horæ," or "Hours," arises from the division of the full day of twenty-four hours into eight periods of three, yet each called an hour. The dedication of special times for prayer is of great antiquity, as is seen by the references to the habits of David, Daniel, Peter and Paul. With the Jews, as with the Romans of later times, the legal day was not from sunrise to sunset, but from eve to eve, and was divided into periods, those of the night being called "watches," and those of the day "hours," each period comprising three ordinary hours. In Horæ, the terms frequently seen are Nocturnes, Matins and Vespers, which indicate, broadly night, morning, and evening services, as the titles "Lauds" or "Matins" do the hours from twelve to three, and from three to six; Prime, six to nine; Tierce, nine to twelve; Sixte, twelve to three; None, three to six; Vespers, six to nine, and Compline or Completorum, nine to twelve.

On the first page of nearly all printed books we are accustomed to see a title which tells the subject, or what it is about, gives the name of the author and the place and date of production. But in manuscript Horæ, especially early ones, there is none of this, and however wishful we may be to know the name of scribe or illuminator, and when or where they worked, they, as a rule, remain unknown, or can only be guessed at from circumstantial evidence. These peculiarities cause the beginning of a Book of Hours to have an appearance of bareness, as if short of a leaf. The reader is met with what at first sight looks like an index, but is really a calendar,* not of astronomical imformation, but giving a list of saints' days and church festivals, varying as they do in different localities. This calendar generally occupies twelve leaves, but sometimes is compressed into half that number, while the text of the book may occupy from one to two hundred leaves, according to the number of services it contains, or the size of the book, which ranges from two inches up to ten. The chief services in most of them are:—The Hours of the Virgin, The Penitential Psalms, The Service for the Dead, and the Litany. The following is Tite's list of the subjects usually found in Books of Hours or offices, though they are not in all, nor in the exact order here given, and there are others occasionally met with which are not here at all.

    1. The Calendar.
    2. Gospels of the Nativity, as given by John, Matthew and Luke, and the Resurrection by Mark.
    3. Preliminary Prayers inserted occasionally.
    4-11. Horæ Beatæ Mariæ Virginis.
        1. Nocturnes and Matins.
        2. Lauds.
        3. Prime.
        4. Tierce.
        5. Sixte.
        6. None.
        7. Vespers.
        8. Compline.

* In this Calendar the days are not numbered from 1 to 30, but in series of seven, marked by letters *a, b, c, &c.*, and also by the old Roman notation of Kalendæ, idus, nonæ. The golden and dominical numbers are also often given. In some calendars the name of a saint is attached to every day, in others there is only a limited number, the more important are in colours or gold.

12. Penitential Psalms.
13. Litany.
14. Horæ Sanctæ Crucis.
15. Horæ De Sancto Spiritu.
16. Officium Defunctorum,
17. Les Quinse Joyes De Nostre Dame.
18. Les Sept Requestes A Nostre Seigneur.
19. Suffragia Plurimorum et Sanctorum.
20. Sequuntur Plures Orationes, Petitiones, etc.

James says a typical Book of Hours ought to contain the following parts, in this order:—

1. Kalendar.
2. Sequentiæ of the Gospels.
3. Hours of the Blessed Virgin.
4. Hours of the Cross.
5. Hours of the Holy Ghost.
6. Seven Penitential Psalms and Litany.
7. Office of the Dead.
8. Memorial or Suffrages to various Saints.

It has already been mentioned that ~~Latin is~~ the language used by Rome in its religous services and official communications, and ~~Horæ~~ also are in that tongue, so pictures were of value, if not absolutely needed, to indicate the services for each hour, and tell in pictorial language the chief incident in the service, in fact to give the same information as pictures did on windows or walls of the church or cathedral, to stimulate piety and to be a foundation for faith. These seem the chief reasons why Horæ are the most profusely illuminated of all books of theology or devotion. The pictures and illuminations on these differ greatly in number and merit, so that every Book of Hours is like an original work. The calendar may be almost plain, or have a brilliant border, in which are indented small pictures. The text of the services may have the initial letters of each, simply coloured, with a few common-place pictures of little artistic value inserted, or the initial letters may be an elaborate composition, of large size, or be like a jewelled frame, holding within it a small miniature. The margin of the text may, on all four sides, be adorned with floral, arabesque, or conventional decorations, enclosing pictorial medallions, while larger pictures, filling the whole or part of an entire page, may appear at the beginning of each service, or of every hour in it. These larger pictures strike the key-note. The same point in the story is taken in all examples. It represents the chief incident on which the service is founded, and in the manner of doing which a certain tradition is generally followed. For instance, in the lessons from the Gospels, with which Horæ generally begin, a portrait of the Evangelists is given, occupied in writing, each being accompanied and assisted by one of the four creatures which are their symbols, the Eagle of St. John, the Lion of St. Mark, the Angel of St. Matthew, and the Ox of St. Luke, while in the Hours of the Virgin, before Nocturne, the incident is nearly always the same, an Angel appearing and announcing to the Virgin the dignity to which she was destined. The scene may be laid in a church, a chamber, or a garden. Wherever it is, the Virgin is usually represented as engaged in prayer, sometimes spinning; occasionally the picture is in two sections, the

Virgin occupied in both ways. In one I possess the annunciation is joined with another representing the marriage.

The second hour, Lauds, represents the Virgin's visit to her cousin Elizabeth; the third hour, Prime, is of the nativity; the fourth, Tierce, the shepherds in the fields; the fifth, Sixte, the offering of the wise men; the sixth, Nones, the presentation in the temple; the seventh, Vespers, the flight into Egypt; the eight, Compline, the massacre of the innocents, or the coronation of the Virgin.

So that, while the text of the Hours of the Virgin consists of prayers, lessons, psalms and hymns, varying slightly in different localities, the miniatures are a pictorial history of the chief recorded events in her life.

Before most of the other services in a Book of Hours there is often but one miniature, even if there be in it a series of eight hours. There is but one before the Penitential Psalms, and it is nearly always some incident in the life of David — killing of Goliath, engaged in prayer, confronted with the three alternatives, or looking from a window at Bathsheba. The latter is never seen excepting in French manuscripts, and is indicative of their nationality. There is not any miniature before the Litany, but the initial letter of every invocation is illuminated. Before the Hours of the Cross there is generally a picture of the crucifixion. Before those of Sancto Spiritu, the descent of the Holy Ghost. Before the service for the dead, or Officium Defunctorum, the miniature may be a service in church, an interment, or the last judgment, while, in one case, a battle is represented. In what is called "Suffragia" there are generally small miniatures of the saints whose aid and services are sought.

From this it will be understood that the bulk of Horæ contain about twelve or fifteen large miniatures, and sometimes a greater number of smaller ones. But in all countries there were Horæ produced for important personages where the number is greatly increased. A Missal written for Charles VI—and what was remarkable, not in Latin, but entirely in French—contains six hundred and fifty six miniatures. The Book of Offices called the Bedford Missal, the work of several artists, was made in France, for John the Duke, brother of our Henry V, and, after his death, Regent of France. It has fifty-nine large miniatures, and in the borders fully one thousand small ones of about one-and-a-half inches each square, while a Breviary of his had forty-five large ones, and was intended to contain between four and five thousand small ones, only about half the number, owing to his death, being completed. The Pembroke Book of Hours, now in America, has about twenty large miniatures and about two hundred and fifty small ones.

In the 15th century, Horæ were deemed so essential in beginning life, that it is probable there were few families of any importance that did not possess one or more. First they were a means of salvation, their use obtaining indulgencies, they were pleasant to the eye as a jewel, and had money value like one. There is a picture by Quentin Matsys where an illuminated manuscript is being sold or pledged for money.

Beyond this they were highly esteemed as the gift of parent, friend, or husband, and accompanied the bride to her new home, and were used to contain the record of important national and family events. So they were rarely alienated, and when such was done, there was note of it, even a legal instrument was sometimes executed, such as is seen in the Bedford Missal, when it passed from the Duke's wife as a present to his nephew, Henry VI of England. In later times, in France, they were used like an album, to receive from friends and relations expressions of respect, devotion, even gallantry. Some of these books were so carefully and elaborately ornamented that years passed before they were finished, or like many of our cathedrals only after a long interval. A Psalter, begun in the 12th century, was only finished when taken up by that munificent patron of art, the Duke de Berri, in the 15th. One prepared as a marriage present by Edward I to his son was, owing to the death of the latter, only completed years afterwards by a different hand, and the Bedford Breviary, owing to the Duke's death, remains unfinished to this day; while the magnificent Book of Hours lately presented to the nation by Lord Malcolm, and which cost his father three thousand pounds, was begun in Italy, in 1490, and not finished until about thirty years afterwards, in Spain, by order of Charles V. What happened to these and many more of importance happened to many of much less value.

I have an Italian Book of Offices: the scribe has finished a prayer for protection in time of plague, "Oratio Tempore

Pestis," and has begun another which has been left incomplete. I have also a French Book of Hours in which there are about thirty-five pictures occupying the page, or nearly so, but out of nearly five hundred small ones, which the borders were intended to contain, very few are finished. The text is comparatively perfect, as well as most of the borders, but the spaces for pictures in them are empty. One or two are even half finished, as if the artist had only just laid down his pencil, which was never to be taken up. These unfinished manuscripts have always a pathetic interest, for we know it was death that, oftener to patron than to scribe, had put his veto on the peaceful and pleasant labour. The history of conspiracies, assassinations, wars and epidemics, told us in the chronicles, or shewn us in the art of the period, as crystallized in the prayer in our litany, "from plague, pestilence, battle, murder, and sudden death, good Lord deliver us," all truly reflect a time when "the reaper called death" was busy, and humanity was falling under his scythe,* literally like grass before the mower, or he was occupied as Holbein and others shew, in calling individually on all in turn, to become his partner and dance with him into the grave. Nor need we wonder that poems or representations of the Dance of Death†

* In 1348, 50,000 died of the plague and were buried in the Charter House Yard, in London; and Sismondi says that "its ravages in the two years, 1348-1350, destroyed three-fifths of the inhabitants of Europe."

† In the middle ages, one or other of the spectres of pestilence, famine, or battle, were ever present before the eyes or imagination, and must have been the main cause of the series of pictures or poems called the Dance of Death which were so universal in the 15th century.

Probably the idea was first in poem or allegory, then when games with figured cards came from the East, life and death made one of them, afterwards

had then a certain fascination, when merely to read the ravages of the plague or black death, even now, causes something of the feeling with which thunder is heard rolling at a distance. There is rarely any representation of the Dance of Death in manuscript Horæ, but it was frequently part of the decorations that adorned the early printed ones, issued in Paris and elsewhere, as it also appeared in the prayer book, printed by Day, and known as Queen Elizabeth's.

Many of the bridges of Germany and Switzerland had them. More than forty years ago I was surprised to stumble unexpectedly on one at Lucerne. One of the earliest is at Basle, set up, it is said, after a visitation of the plague there. London, Salisbury, and Hexham had them, though for various reasons, national character, freedom from foreign enemies, etc., they never could have been so numerous, or to the same extent, as on the Continent. I am not aware of any ever having been in Ireland or Scotland, but R. L. Stevenson

to be introduced in churches as a pious spectacle, or scenic representation, accompanied with music and dance, ultimately receiving the name of Todten tanz, Danse Macabre—Dance of Death—though in religious matters the term would have the meaning of "procession"—in military matters be like "parade." The first known pictoral representation of the Danse Macabre was placed in the cemetery of the Church of the Innocents, at Paris, in 1424, and the effect of the pictures was deepened by preaching, continued for months, on the lessons they indicated. Such paintings spread and obtained a popularity and universality which has been compared to the almanacks of our time. A French author says, "Every country, every church, every convent wanted to have its Dance of Death in painting, sculpture and tapestry. The subject, funereal and burlesque, frightened the great, consoled and amused the poor; artists of every kind never tired of producing it, in every shape and on every occasion, and it is even found in the engraving on ladies' jewellery."

says "the Scotch stand highest among nations in the matter of grimly illustrating death." "Every mason was a pedestrian Holbein, he had a deep consciousness of death, and lived to put its terrors pithily before the churchyard loiterers." There is no doubt but that in France the national distress and depression following Agincourt, of which the battle of Vergneuil was the climax, seemed to destroy the last hope of national existence—aided by the continual preaching that in death and the grave was the only respite from misery—and invest these representations with a kind of fascination. As the battle of Vergneuil * was as fatal to their allies, the Scots,

* The battle of Vergneuil took place 17th August, 1424, and in it were four or five thousand Scotch combatants, of which one thousand were noblemen. The loss of the battle was attributed to a misunderstanding between them and the French, which prevented them acting in unison. To this and the imprudence of Earl Douglas, the Scotch commander, in refusing to give or accept quarter must their great loss be attributed. A contemporary writer says "it was a fearful spectacle to contemplate the mountain of corpses heaped on the battle field, especially where the struggle with the Scotch took place, as not one of them was taken prisoner. The cause of this merciless carnage was the confidence, "fierté," of the Scotch. Before the engagement the Duke of Bedford, the English commander, sent to ask the Scotch on what conditions they were to fight, and received from Earl Douglas the reply, that on that day they would neither take any prisoners nor be taken. This answer caused their extermination. It is curious to read the French author saying "This check turned to the advantage of France, for such was the pride (orgueil) of the Scotch, and the contempt in which they held the French, that if they had emerged victors out of the struggle, they would have conspired to cut off the nobles of Anjou, Touraine and adjoining provinces, and take possession of all belonging to them of value, which would certainly not have been difficult if they had conquered the English, which they expected doing."—*Les Ecossais en France*, par FRANCISQUE-MICHIL.

Pinkerton says "It was much more certain that the disastrous day of Vergneuil cut short for ever expeditions of Scotch auxiliary troops into France, where they were never more seen beyond a small number of adventurers and some troops during the reigns of James III and IV."

it is not improbable it made an impression which found expression by the mason's chisel. This, no doubt, was guided and directed by national feeling springing, as did the Dance of Death with the French, out of events such as Bannockburn, Flodden, and Drumclog, which in such a country as Scotland, impressed on its religion and literature the seriousness, pathos, and humour by which they are so distinguished.

The only Scottish churchyard I remember being in—which was very long ago—was that of Burns' Alloway Kirk. I was not struck with what Stevenson mentions, but I was with what I had not noticed in England—that the implements used in his trade by the occupier of the grave were often carved on the stone placed over his remains. But that the Scotch should act as Stevenson says might be quite expected from a national character that has given "Old Mortality," "The Cottar's Saturday Night," and "Auld Nickie-ben," which, though only pictures in words, seem to have as distinct a personality, and to be destined to as great permanency, as the figures of Holbein.

EXAMPLES OF ILLUMINATIONS ON BOOKS OF HOURS.

As supplementary to what has been said about Books of Hours, and as aid to make them more intelligible, I now add some examples of the miniatures, etc., on them, which, though without the charm which richness and variety of colour impart to the originals, will, I hope, make the idea obtained of them more complete than any that could possibly be given by words alone.

The frontispiece is from a manuscript, where it appears before the prayer to the Virgin beginning *Obsecro te Domino.* Plate II is the first of twenty-four such pages of a calendar, with which nearly all Books of Hours open. Then, from three different books, are miniatures such as appear at the beginning of the text. These are followed by twelve miniatures from the Hours of the Virgin, the first five, each from a different manuscript, before the first hour, and one each before the other seven. After these come two miniatures that precede isolated prayers to the Virgin, to which succeed others before the Penitential Psalms, the Service for the Dead, the Hours of the Holy Spirit, The Holy Cross, and before Suffragia, or prayers to saints. These twenty-six miniatures are taken from among about two hundred, in twelve different manuscripts, which were produced chiefly in the 15th century, and in France, the time and country of their greatest production.

The Calendar and several subsequent illustrations are taken from a manuscript produced about 1400, when the background of the miniatures was of a diaper or mosaic pattern, and the border was of the kind called ivy leaf. Such backgrounds to miniatures seem not to have been a native development, but to have come into use in the art of the West suddenly, as if taken bodily from Greek examples, perhaps brought by the Crusaders from Constantinople, where the domes of Saint Sophia had been elaborately decorated by Justinian with scriptural figures in brilliant mosaic. What is called the ivy leaf pattern (it is as much like the leaf of the thorn or holly) seems to have begun in shoots or flourishes thrown off from initial letters. Then they were extended, and made to run up or down the outside margin, and ultimately to surround the entire text and miniature, and be a frame for both, for which the pattern was admirably fitted by flexibility and grace. It was in use, and very popular, for about a century, and at the time of the writing of this was perfectly developed. The existence of a mosaic background to miniatures and an ivy leaf pattern of border, help to fix the date of any manuscript in which they appear. This is one of those, more common in early times than later, which was the production of one hand, as it is one of the few in which there is any clue to the name of the scribe and illuminator, or of his patron for whom he worked. Though the two simple words at the end, "Johannes Parvi," say little, yet the researches of Bradly, in his work, *Dictionary of Miniaturists*, make it almost certain he was a native of Brittany, and worked between 1380 and 1420. Though he gives his own name he does not give that of his patron, but he gives what was no doubt sufficient and plain enough then, though at this distance of time we can only reasonably infer that it was Charles VI of France.

It has been named that the ivy leaf pattern decorates the borders, but to the twelve leaves of the calendar of this manuscript it is seen by this example:—there is an outside border of golden rays which, issuing from the "sun in its splendour" in the four corners, meet in the middle of the ends and outer edge. This may seem, at first sight, merely an effective

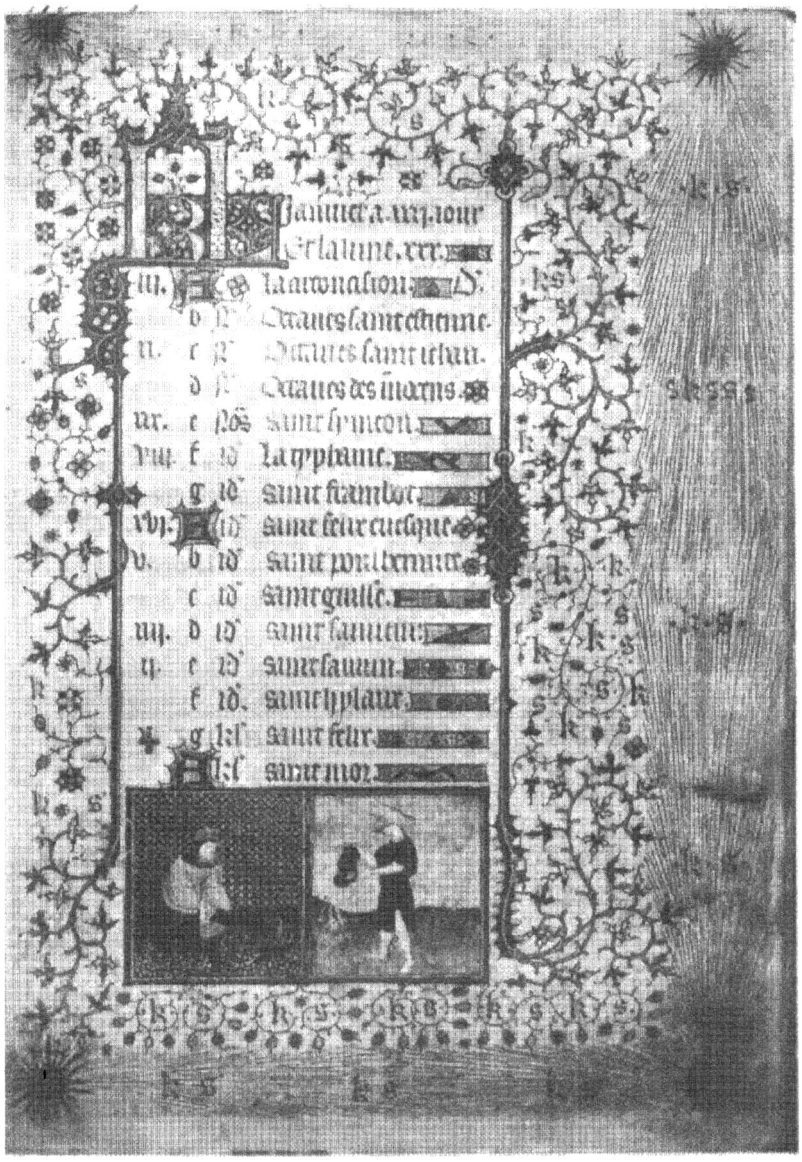

Beginning of a Calendar—French, 1400.

additional decoration. It was that, and more, being a personal badge assumed by the owner, differing from device on shield or armour, which was that of the family, and it gives a clue as to who was the owner. The "sun in its splendour" was a badge adopted by Charles VI,[*] as it was three hundred years afterwards by Louis XIV, who, from that circumstance, is sometimes called "King Sun;" and Versailles, which he founded, the home of "Roi soleil." Further confirmation is in the circumstance that throughout the calendar, and at various pages at the end of the manuscript, two letters, "𝕂. 𝕊.,"[†] are abundantly introduced: about

[*] Froissart says that one of the devices of Charles VI, at the tournament on the entry of Queen Isabella, was a sun. There were thirty knights, including the king, who styled themselves Knights of the Golden Sun, each bearing on his shield a splendid sun.

[†] It will be noted that the letters 𝕂. 𝕊. on this calendar are such as our printers call "Old English," but the French call an S of this form, where an oblique line unites the two points, S fermé, S barré, or closed S. It is found a century later on French bindings, and its meaning there has given rise to many inquiries. In works on Bindings it may be shown by examples, and the fact named, but without comment. The only attempt at explanation is in a work, "*Monogrammes Historiques*, par Aglaüs Bouvenne," in which he says: "Quant à l' S barré, c'est-à-dire traversé d'un simple trait, c'est encore un jeu de mots qui signifie souvent *Fermesse, Fermete*." In this calendar the S fermé is preceded and connected with the letter K, and they are of equal size, and doubtless together mean "Karolus Sextus." The binding is later than the manuscript, and on it the S barré appears, but at the angles, smaller, and, like satellites, surrounding a monogram, which is the Greek letter λ interlaced. On bindings that is the form and position usually seen, always smaller, and surrounding the monogram or initials of the individual, and never with the arms of the family. In one case it is seen on the books of an abbess, with her monogram, while her brother, an abbé, on his books, has the arms of his father, without any S fermé. If I may venture an opinion, it is that its place on bindings had some connection with the use of the SS gold collar, and was only on the books of those entitled to wear that as part of their costume. The SS collar

thirty times it may be counted on the page here given, and in the entire volume about five hundred times.* These doubtless stand for Karolus Sextus. There is some corroboration in the introduction of the *fleur-de-lys* in several of the borders, though, did that stand alone, it would be of little importance. This illustration (Plate II) is given not only on account of its being an unusual, and, as far as I know, unique decoration, but to show the kind of appearance of the calendars attached to Books of Hours, which often have two small miniatures of the occupations of the month, and the signs of the Zodiac. After the calendar,

had a religious origin, but in time came to be associated with secular dignity. Randle Holme says: "It was the Knights' enseigns—denoting them to be Sirs—that is, Heroes, or great Lords." Several instances are mentioned where, on the creation of a knight, he was invested with an SS collar. It is now, and has been for long, attached to some offices and worn by the holder, *ex officio*, as by the Lord Mayor of London. But in earlier times it was a personal dignity appertaining to the individual, and valued, as is evident by its appearance on statuary portraits on tombs, of which several may be seen in the Cheshire churches of Cheadle, Mottram, Malpas, and Macclesfield. In one case—a Mainwaring—not only the knight, but also his lady, is represented wearing it; so it seems not unlikely that those entitled to wear the SS collar might wish to indicate the honour on the binding of their books, as, in addition to his initial or badge, a king often placed a crown; the pope, his tiara; a cardinal, his hat; and the bishop, his mitre or crozier; and thus made it serve, with his monogram, in lieu of family arms, for a bookplate, if it be not the earliest form of one. Why S fermé was preferred to SS, may simply be because shorter, more decorative, and going better with the monogram, while also in harmony with the practice of making a horizontal or oblique line to indicate an abbreviation. This may or may not be the true explanation, and is offered in the absence of any other.

* Bouvenne says Missals made for kings, queens, princes of the church, or some lords who could afford the exceptional luxury, were often ornamented with the monogram of the personage who ordered them, or for whom they were destined.

Initium sancti euangelii secundum
Johannem. In principio erat uerbum, et uerbum
erat apud deum, et deus erat uerbum. Hoc

Plate III.

St. John in Patmos—French, 1400.

Plate IV.

St. John in Patmos—French, 1450.

St. John, and also Expulsion from Eden--French, 1475.

a Book of Hours, especially early ones, opens quite abruptly, without any titlepage, as is evident in the two given (Plates III and IV), which are the beginning of the Gospel of St. John. This is usually followed, as in these, by those from Matthew and Luke, and also by Mark's description of Christ's appearance to the eleven after his resurrection. Each of these extracts from the respective gospels has usually a miniature representing the apostle engaged in writing the account given, as these miniatures do.

The miniature (Plate IV) is the same subject from another French manuscript, where a landscape is the background, and the borders, and treatment generally, are quite different. The third (Plate V) is the same subject from a still later manuscript, where St. John, writing, is united with the expulsion from Eden, bringing together the last and first books of the Bible—the Apocalypse and Genesis. This appears at the end of St. Mark's account (xvi, 14), and indicates a further change in the borders. After these extracts from the Gospels, called *sequentia*—sometimes before them—there are generally prayers to the Virgin, without any miniatures; but three are given—one, the Frontispiece; the others, Plates XVIII and XIX.

Most frequently after the *sequentia* comes the special service called "Hours of the Virgin," and its division into eight sections, each as a rule having a miniature at the beginning, of which the first is called Nocturnes or Matins, the time for saying which is 9 p.m. to 12, and 12 to 3 a.m. The miniature before this is nearly always the annunciation, and the one given

(Plate VI) from the earliest manuscript is a good example, and in every respect characteristic of the art of the period.

Another of the same subject is from a manuscript of a rather later period (Plate VII), chosen to indicate the change that time has made in decoration. The mosaic background is retained, but the border is not so purely ivy leaf pattern, the acanthus and other forms being introduced. This is smaller in size, it contains fewer services, only thirteen miniatures, and the calendar is plain. The text begins with the two hymns to the Virgin, and there are not any miniatures before them or before the extracts from the Gospels, and the text is without borders in the ordinary sense. Yet the colours of the thirteen miniatures are very brilliant, the bright blue and red, so characteristic of French Horæ of this time, and a sign of nationality, being very apparent. The next example (Plate VIII) is of the same subject, from a Flemish manuscript, which the late Sir W. Tite, to whom it belonged, described as of the middle of the 15th century. A great contrast is seen here between the style of this and the two last miniatures. There is an approach to a title page, which states it to be the form of Horæ used by the Carthusians, who were opposed to luxuriousness in the use of art, either on books or in churches. Here the Virgin is in her chamber, and a small figure in Carthusian costume indicates the miniature was a votive offering. This manuscript is without any calendar, nor are there any borders excepting surrounding the miniature and the opposite page. These borders are different from any yet given, being detached flowers and fruit, with

The Annunciation—French, 1400.

The Annunciation—French, 1400.

Plate VII.

The Annunciation — French, 1425.

The Annunciation, etc., open book—Flemish, 1450.

Plate VIII.

The Annunciation, etc., open book—Flemish, 1450.

Plate X.

The Annunciation, etc., open book—Italian, 1475.

The Visitation, etc., open book.—Flemish, 1450.

Plate XII.

The Nativity, with Wise Men on Journey — French, 1475.

birds and insects on a gold ground. To show the difference in style, an example of the same subject (Plate IX) is given from an Italian Book of Hours still smaller. The colours employed are different from any preceding, and the borders contain medallions of beautifully drawn human figures. Another of the same nationality (Plate X) has a different border, the ground being like worm marks in gold, and the medallions containing birds and animals. This is assumed to be the work of some artist of Sienna.

The second service in the Hours of the Virgin was from 3 to 6 a.m., called Lauds, and is usually preceded by a representation of the visit of the Virgin to her cousin Elizabeth. The one given (Plate XI) is taken from the Flemish manuscript, the scene being in the open country, where, though on a small scale, the power and truth of its delineation, both of distance and foreground, and the delicate colours employed, are "true to nature, and pleasing to the eye," which De Gray Birch says were characteristic of that school.

The third service, called Prime, has usually a representation of the nativity. The one here given (Plate XII) is from a manuscript where it was introduced, not in this order, but before St. Matthew's description of this event, and is from an unfinished French manuscript, which was intended to contain two small miniatures on the borders of every page throughout the book. Had it been completed on that scale it would have contained about 500 such as here seen, of the Magi on their journey, and their arrival "where the young child was," of which a representation is shewn in the large miniature.

The fourth service, called Tierce, has before it the shepherds in the fields. The one chosen (Plate XIII) is from the Flemish manuscript.

The fifth service, called Sixte, has the wise men, or Magi, making their offering, and the plate (XIV) is from the Charles VI manuscript.

The sixth, called Nones, has the representation of the presentation in the Temple. This, as well as the next example (Plates XV and XVI), are from a small French manuscript of the late date of 1516, previously stated to have been injured by water.

The seventh is called Vespers, and has the miniature of the flight into Egypt. The borders of these two, it is seen, are architectural.

The eighth service is called Compline, or Completorium, for it completes the round of the twenty-four hours. The miniature preceding it is usually either one representing the Massacre of the Innocents, or the Coronation of the Virgin. The one given (Plate XVII) is of the latter, taken from the Flemish Book of Hours, the border being architectural, the one on the opposite page being adoring angels in " Camaïeu gris."* In most of the Hours of the Virgin there are miniatures before the various services in it, but the prayers to her beginning " Obsecro de Domino," and composed by St.

* This is the title given to miniatures in which only two colours are used, white and gray. In some Books of Hours they are entirely of those colours. As this is one according to Carthusian usage, there is a propriety in using these colours, seeing that in staining the windows of its churches that order used no others.

Plate XIII.

The Shepherds in the Fields, etc., open book—Flemish, 1450.

Plate XIV.

The Visit of the Wise Men—French, 1400.

Plate XV.

The Presentation in the Temple—French, 1516.

Title-page of Euclid, 1507.

Plate XVI.

The Flight into Egypt—French 1516.

Plate XVII.

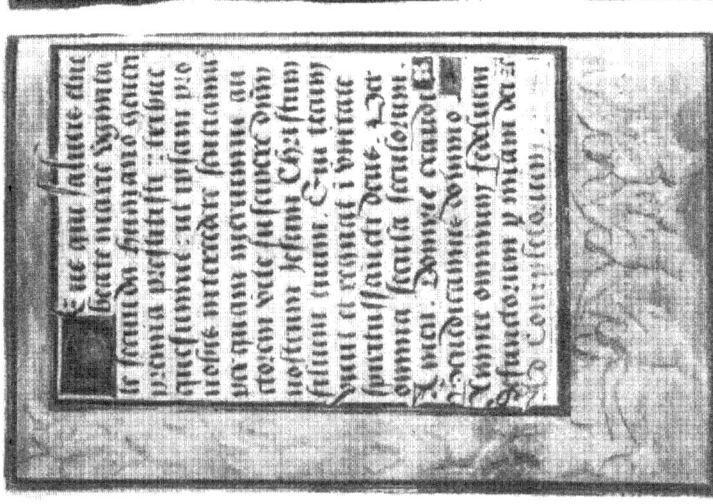

The Coronation of the Virgin, etc., open book—Flemish, 1450.

Plate XVIII.

The Virgin and Child—French, 1400.

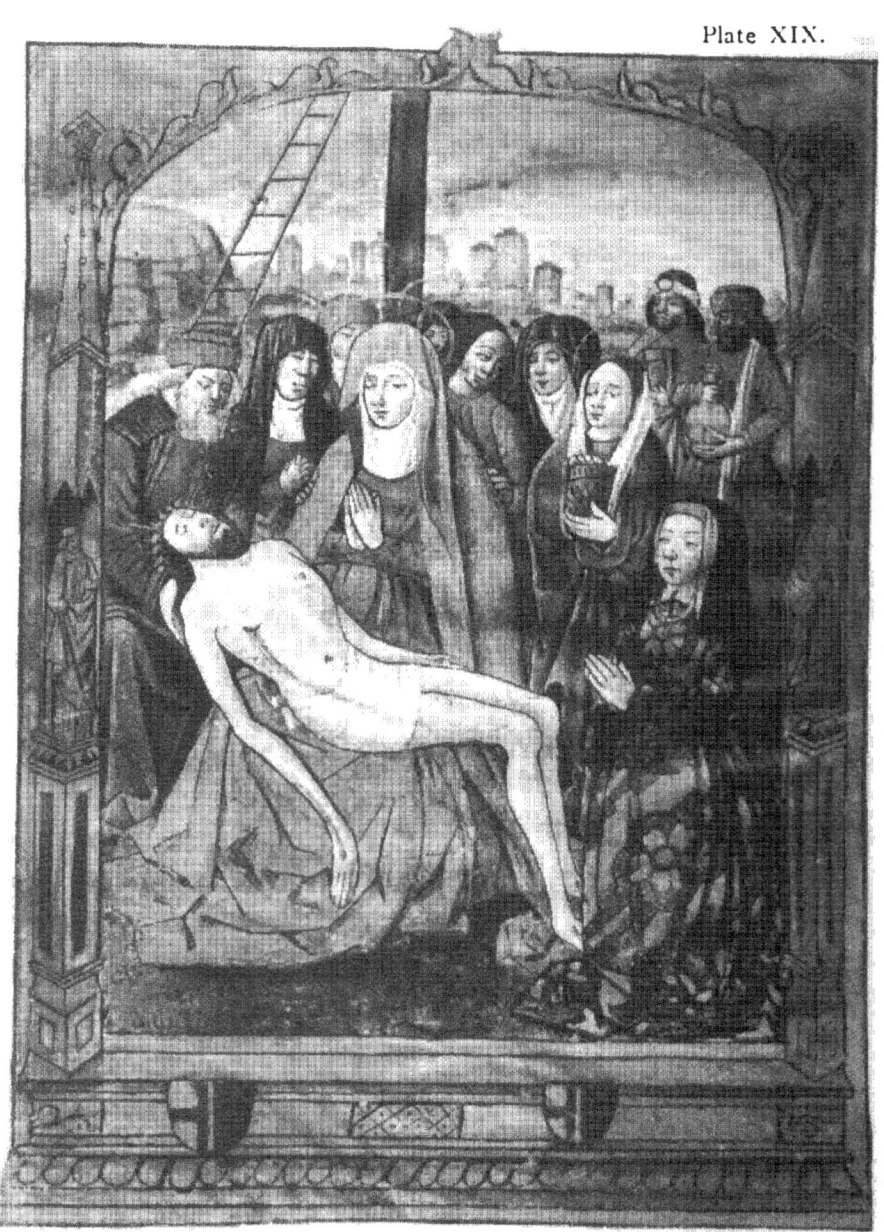

Stabat Mater—French, 1450.

Plate XX.

Penitence of David — French, 1475.

Service for the Dead, by Choir at Vespers—French, 1450.

Battle—French, 1475.

Plate XXIII.

Descent of the Holy Ghost—French, 1450.

PLATE XXVII.

Descent of Holy Ghost. French. 1450.

Edmund, Archbishop of Canterbury, "O intemerata" and the "Stabat Mater," miniatures are not so often seen. Of the first of these prayers I give examples from two different French manuscripts to shew the different treatment of the same subject and the change in style during the seventy or eighty years that separated them. The earlier one is Plate XVIII, and the later one is the Frontispiece. A miniature before the Stabat Mater is also given on Plate XIX. The shield at the bottom is that of the family for which the manuscript was produced, and the lady kneeling before the group which surrounds the body, just taken from the cross, is an important member of it, and is represented in the habit as she lived.

Before the Penitential Psalms the miniature given (Plate XX) of David kneeling in the court of a Norman castle, is from a manuscript produced probably about 1500, in the town of Mons. This circumstance was made known to me by Mr. Weale, who found in the calendar the name of a saint peculiar to the locality. The miniature before the service for the dead may represent Job in his affliction, burial in a cemetery, or the service in a church. The latter is given (Plate XXI) as well as one from another French manuscript, which is what is rarely represented in this connection, a battle (Plate XXII).

Before the Hours of the Holy Spirit the miniature (Plate XXIII) is from a French manuscript, much injured by use, mainly, I think, in Italy, for the binding is that of an Italian family, and there are services added in a later Italian hand.

The scribe and the miniaturist must, in this case, have been different persons. On each miniature the artist has added his initials, P. L., and, in one border, his name in full. The Christian name, Petrus, is plain, but what looks like L a s s u s is less so. Attached to this is the date MCCCIII, repeated in a later hand at the end. The style of decoration is a century later, so there is probably an error in this date.

Before the Hours of the Holy Cross, in the Charles VI manuscript, there are miniatures before each of the seven hours, viz.:—The Betrayal, Before Pilate, Bearing the Cross, Crucifixion, Death, Descent, Burial, which latter is given (Plate XXIV).

Most Books of Hours end with what is called Suffragia, or Prayers to Saints, there may be two or three or twenty or more. They are accompanied in many cases by a small miniature, in which either their mode of martyrdom is shewn or the performance of some miracle attributed to them. The miniature (Plate XXV) here given is from the same manuscript as the last, and is of the apostles Peter and Paul, each having the emblem connected with him, the keys and sword. These dignified figures recall those of Leonardi da Vinci in the celebrated picture of the last supper.

These named are the chief services found in ordinary Books of Hours, but there are others met with in certain books in addition or in lieu of those named, for there is no rule as to what a Book of Hours should contain, nor in what order they should come. But when these others appear, miniatures are not so generally an accompaniment as with the

Plate XXIV.

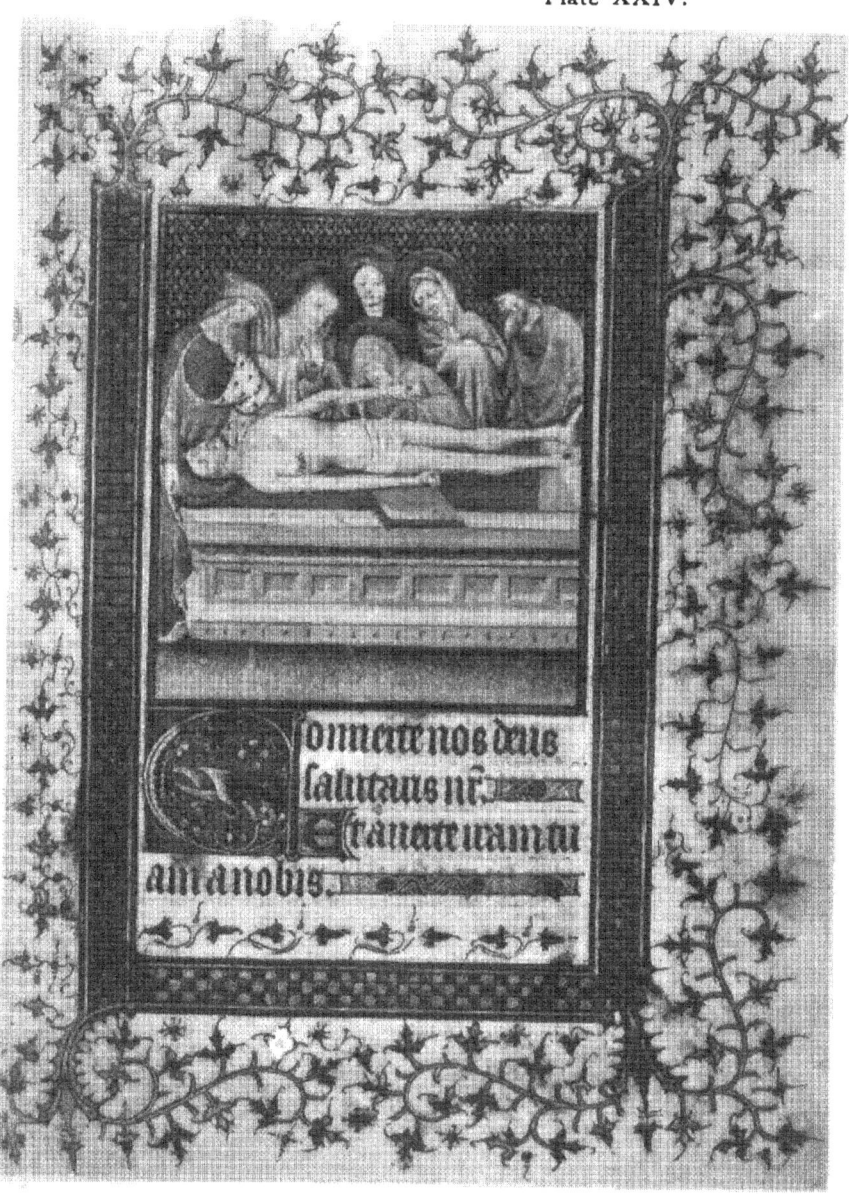

Burial of Christ—French, 1400.

Saints Peter and Paul — French, 1400.

Plate XXVI.

Death and Ascension of the Virgin—Italian, 1500.

services already named. The following, it may be noted, are sometimes met with:—

The Hours or Office of the Assumption of B. V. Mary—
       „   „   the Compassion of B. V. M.
       „   „   the Name of Jesus.
       „   „   the Passion of our Lord.
       „   „   the Eternal Wisdom.
       „   „   Saint Francis.
       „   „   All Saints.
       „   „   the Holy Sacrament.

The Psalter of St. Jerome.
The Prayer, "Salve Regina."
The XV Prayers of St. Birgitta of Sweden (called the XV OO's in English Horæ).
The Athanasian Creed.
The VII Prayers of St. Gregory.
The Verses of St. Bernard.
The Prayer of St. Augustine.
The Prayer of Venerable Bede.

I give one miniature (Plate XXVI) from the first of them, mainly to shew an Italian border, very graceful, that was frequently used not only in manuscripts, but was sometimes applied by hand to the first page of early printed books, making them look greatly like manuscripts.

The Books of Hours from which the examples are taken were obtained twenty or thirty years ago. They are scarcer now, especially such as the two which supply Plates II, III, and VI, also VIII, XIII, and XVII.

The one from which the three latter are taken formed part of the excellent collection of the late Sir W. Tite, who personally described it as being "of the best Flemish art of the period;" and the other the late Professor Westwood thought was one of what he called the "Royal Books" of France, and, from the art exhibited in it, he considered it not unworthy of being classed with the "Grandes Heures" of the Duc de Berri. Apart from art, it is of some interest that the King of France, Charles VI, for whom it was made was father of the Kate, whose wooing and winning by our Henry V, as given by Shakespeare in his play of that name, is such a contrast and so amusing an episode after the stirring events of Agincourt. As can be understood by those acquainted with illuminated manuscripts, all the examples here given are deprived of much of their charm through colour being eliminated. Black is a poor substitute for red, blue, green, or gold, in combination or contrast, and the difference to the eye is as great as a garden of flowers in the daytime, and the same seen by the light of a clouded moon.

Yet these various examples, denuded though they be of their natural accompaniments, will give an idea, however imperfect, of the miniatures which, with their complement of borders and initial letters, united in making a good Book of Hours a very beautiful and interesting object, precious at the time for many reasons, and even now satisfactory from a merely decorative point of view, to which all the parts, including the mere writing, contributed. Crane, the great authority on decorative art, says "The page of a Book of Hours, in fact, may be regarded as a flat panel, which may be variously spaced out. The calligrapher, the illuminator, and the miniaturist, are the architects who planned out their vellum grounds and built beautiful structures of line and colour upon them for thought and fancy to dwell in;" that "a prayer book was not only a prayer book, but a picture book, a shrine, a little mirror of the world, a sanctuary in a garden of flowers."

Conclusion.

In bringing these desultory and fragmentary remarks to a conclusion, it but remains to guard against leaving the impression that all Books of Hours are such as Crane's true description of some, or that all illuminations possess artistic merit, and that copies of the sacred writings, or any selections from them, or decorations on them, were always the outcome of high motives. It must be admitted that the motive was sometimes that of a hireling, sordid enough, and that the art applied was indifferent, or actually poor. Yet there are very few illuminated manuscripts destitute of interest, antiquarian or otherwise, while the best of them touch human nature in many points, and is explanation of the charm they possess, and the estimation in which they are held. In such the artists seem to have done their best, and it is the best art of the time, and, in some manuscripts, it is equal to that of any time. The pictures and decorations are not only a pleasure in themselves, but they enable the imagination to realise, as not anything else does, the life and manners of a time, long past, which are the foundations on which our own rest, the roots and stock from which they have sprung. These manuscripts have also a human interest, greatly absent from printed books, that every line and ornament on them was traced by some hand, now centuries in the dust, and the skilful, patient, or pious labour seldom appeals in vain for respect or admiration. They are also often personal relics, inferior to none in dignity, of men and women who played a part on the world's stage, and whose story is ever new and interesting to each succeeding generation. Among many that might be named are the saints Columba and Augustine, the scholars Theodore and Alcuin, the Kings Alfred * and Charlemagne,† with many of their successors, Louis the saint,‡ and Louis the unfortunate, as well as our own Edwards, and Harrys, and the four daughters and grand-daughters—Queens all—of the victor of Bosworth Field.‖ As we look on their books of relaxation or devotion,

* We all know the story that it was an illuminated manuscript by which the mother of the Great Alfred attracted and bound him for ever to art and literature. It has long disappeared, for reasons we can easily understand, and for the fact, there may not be evidence that would satisfy Euclid or Blackstone, but there is what would have satisfied Shakespeare, or anyone with knowledge of human nature, as something similar has often enough happened in humbler life.

† Charlemagne had a knowledge and delight in art equal to our Charles I He had an illuminated manuscript buried with him.

‡ St. Louis, according to Mr. Morley, one of the only two perfect Princes recorded in history, founded one of the first libraries in France, gave it some of his own books, and came there to study them like a private gentleman.

The last earthly possession of his successor, Louis XVI, a thousand years afterwards, was a small illuminated prayer book, that he only parted with on the scaffold. As it was by the celebrated calligraphist Jarry, and an instance of the instability of human greatness, I was anxious for its possession, and a few years ago attended its sale in London. To the bookseller who obtained it I, unavailingly, offered an enhanced price.

‖ Henry VII had two daughters, Queen Margaret of Scotland, and Mary of France, and grand-daughters, Mary and Elizabeth of England. He appears in

and turn over leaves, or linger over pictures they have done, history becomes a reality, and events and figures in it rise unbidden, and pass before us silently in long procession, and if, standing as we do on higher ground, in point of time, we consider the generations that have gone, it creeps in upon us that our own must soon fall in and follow on. We realise that our time and generation will soon be linked on to the great chain of human existence, and come up before posterity for judgment. What it will look like, or how appear, we may not say. If, like many before, it be marked by earthly stains, rust or dust, we should remember that as each of us live, we may add to them, or help, that from under or in spite of them, may shine a kindly light, cheering to patriotism and an aid to piety, which, Dr. Johnson said, "is ever strengthened on the plains of Marathon and warmed amid the ruins of Iona."

history as austere, and having iron nerves, but a Missal given by him to his daughter Margaret exhibits him in a milder light. In one place he wrote on it: "Remember your kynde and Lovying fader in yo'r good prayers." And in another place—"Pray for your lovying fader that gave you this book;" and "I give att all times Godds blessing and mine." Both these are signed HENRY R., in letters which, in size and distinctness, stand out and above the text as King Saul did among his subjects.

The subsequent history of this manuscript is better known than that of many. It passed from Henry's grand-daughter as a gift to the Archbishop of St. Andrew's. He took it on to the Continent, and for a century it was in private hands at Bruges. The death of the owner caused its sale to General Wade, from whom it passed, again by gift, to the Earl of Burlington, and so to the Duke of Devonshire, in whose family it is now and has been for nearly two hundred years.

www.ingramcontent.com/pod-product-compliance
Lightning Source LLC
Chambersburg PA
CBHW031352230426
43670CB00006B/516